DEAR WOMAN

DEAR WOMAN

Written By: Michael E. Reid
Edited by: Meloni C. Williams

Dreams On Paper Entertainment Publishing
PHILADELPHIA

Also by Michael E. Reid

The Boyfriend Book
Just Words
Just Words 2

Mango Publishing Group
2850 Douglas Road, 3rd Floor
Coral Gables, FL 33134 USA
info@mango.bz

For special orders, quantity sales, course adoptions and corporate sales, please email the publisher at sales@mango.bz. For trade and wholesale sales, please contact Ingram Publisher Services at customer.service@ingramcontent.com or +1.800.509.4887.

Library of Congress Cataloging
ISBN: (print) 978-1-63353-839-9 (ebook) 978-1-63353-840-5
Library of Congress Control Number: 2018952295
BISAC category code: POE023020 POETRY / Subjects & Themes / Love & Erotica, FAM029000 FAMILY & RELATIONSHIPS / Love & Romance

Printed in the United States of America

This book is dedicated to every woman I have ever met.
Some for minutes, some for months, some forever.
I listened. I thought. I wrote.

---

*"No matter how many times the world changes
what it means to be a woman, you
never stop being a woman in it."*

This Book Belongs To:

Dear Woman,

This is YOUR book.
With it comes the responsibility to be a better woman.
Also a better friend, a better daughter, a better mother, a
better wife.
Not everything will apply.
What does: take with you for the rest of your life.
What doesn't: make sure it never will apply.
This book comes with an obligation—
An obligation to not only be a better woman
but, also, to build better women around you.
Do not take this duty lightly.
One day, your daughter will need friends.
Someday, your son will need a wife.
The best way to make sure they have the best opportunities to
find beautiful women is for you to do your part in helping to
build them.
May these words bring you great pleasure, great peace, and
great hope.

Respectfully,

Michael E. Reid

Table of Contents

Foreword

Today is June 1, 2018, and it has been exactly three years, five months, and eighteen days since I originally released *Dear Woman*. Words cannot express the gratitude and humility I feel after receiving some of the testimonials from its readers. You are surely in for a treat. Thank you so much to everyone who has messaged me on social media, emailed, and stopped me on the street. All of your kind words and heartfelt praise are the fuel that still keeps my fire burning all these years later.

While we have a few pages before you get into my work, let me tell you a bit about myself. First, obviously you know my name is Mike. As I type this, I am a thirty-three-year-old African American male from Philadelphia, Pennsylvania. I am a proud product of a single-parent household. I was fortunate enough to have witnessed the struggle of watching a mother try to provide for her children alone at first hand. So, to those women who are currently living in that truth: I see you, I love you, and I pray for you daily.

I also have a younger sibling whom I love very much. My sister Charlonda is about four years younger than me, so in addition to being raised by a woman, I also had the amazing opportunity of attempting to assist in raising one. These responsibilities, which while growing up felt like handicaps to my own personal growth and development, are the pillars on which I stand today.

Witnessing those experiences firsthand: a father walking out on his children, a woman attempting to process and accept an unsuccessful marriage, a daughter trying to grasp why her father isn't around anymore, were pains that I eventually turned into a beautiful purpose. So, to those who are struggling with pain today: fear not, for what you do with that pain can turn burdens into blessings.

I was in the third grade when my father left. Domestic violence, drug abuse, alcoholism, and infidelity were the wedges that drove my parents apart. Talking to my mother years later, when I felt we were both mature enough and healed enough to have a real conversation about it, she said, "Maybe if there were only one or two battles to fight, it could have worked." Unfortunately, having so many holes in the armor of their marriage left her in a position of hopelessness. But instead of being the final nail in the coffin of her attempt at love and family, that hopelessness became a seed. A seed that our "new" family planted and watered daily with love, strength, God, and each other.

I did my best to be a good son—with a few bumps and bruises along the way, most of which were inflicted by my mom. At 5'5", sometimes she felt as if the only way she could discipline her 6'2" 180-pound "man-child" was with an iron fist—and sometimes even an ironing board. This proved to be useful to a point. Eventually her discipline shifted to tough love by way of cutting her strings of support. As I got older, I was faced with having to fend for myself for the things I wanted. If I was grown enough to skip school, talk back, and miss curfew, I was old enough to learn how to provide for myself.

This form of discipline was tougher than any "beating" she ever gave me, but it was what most certainly catapulted me into manhood. I started off with summer jobs at the age of thirteen that continued through high school. By seventeen, as a senior, I was splitting my time between classes and a part-time job at McDonalds. Eventually, I had my first dance with the law; that put my dreams of being a nurse like my mother to the side. Two months before my eighteenth birthday, I found myself in Great Lakes, Illinois, with a shaved head, in sweatpants with no pockets. My juvenile status as a defendant coupled with my father's influence as one of the most respected social workers in the city (how ironic) left me with the options of either being put through a series of rehabilitation services in Philadelphia or joining the military.

My 3.3 grade point average and SAT score of 1220 out of a possible 1600 gave me the option to choose which branch of the military I wanted to join. I chose the Navy. This was such a huge stepping stone in my elevation into manhood. The military taught me all the things that my mother didn't, and that my father didn't want to. To all those reading this who have also served our country, I offer my salute. To all the mothers looking for ways to rescue their own "man-child" from the ways of the world and of the streets, I would take a strong look at the military. The sense of honor, courage, and commitment to myself, as well as to something bigger than me, proved so useful to me and my future.

Fast-forwarding a little, after five years of award-winning military service, I found myself back in Philadelphia. My heart was set on pursuing my education as a healthcare professional and being the big brother and son that my family needed. That was the plan, until I had the bright idea of falling in love.

I have always been drawn to women, more so than to sports, school, hobbies, or video games. Growing up in the inner city in the '90s, street corners were peppered with young men. I was in the house. Cooking, cleaning, doing laundry—truly a renaissance man in the making. My mother's schedule—student by day, nurse by night—left me with a lot of free time, time that I used to invite girls over. I thought it was cool that I could show off my culinary skills and attentiveness to them. They rewarded me with praise for my "from scratch" alfredo sauce as well as for my desire to hear all about their goals and dreams. As you can see, even at a young age, my desire to cater to women came long before my ability to write.

Writing came later. In the fall of 2011, I was three years into the most fascinating, heartbreaking, roller-coaster ride of my adult life to this day. I was in love. I was head over heels for the woman who for all three years of our relationship I thought that I was going to spend the rest of my life with. That feeling lasted right up until the day before I planned to propose. When we met, we were both college students, both broke, and both madly in love with each other. We spent 360 out of our first 365 days as a couple together. We made sacrifices for love almost daily. My dropping out of school to support our relationship and her being faced with the ultimatum of choosing between her mother's rules and our love left us both giving up our pasts for our future. I wasn't the man then that I am today. Immaturity, lack of guidance in the world of relationships, and the smothering type of love I gave ultimately put our fire out.

We loved each other enough to try and keep lighting the fire, though. The last few months of our relationship were a "Groundhog Day" set of attempts to rekindle the flame. But eventually, and unfortunately, the tears from the pain we caused each other made the wood too moist to catch fire. In a last-ditch effort to save our love for good, I took the remainder of my savings and bought a ring. It was too little, too late.

While I was trying to figure out the direction of my life, she pressed on and finished school. Her desire to practice law had been evident early on—the arguments we had as a couple were proof. Ultimately, the stress of trying to save a relationship while trying for a high GPA left her with few options for law school. To this day, I still take much of the blame. Fearful that her leaving to go to school in a remote place would prove deadly to our relationship, I planned to propose and make one last stand for our love. Unfortunately, I was a day late.

The day before I planned to propose, she took me to our favorite park, the same park where we would go for walks, have picnics, and even joke about having our wedding there. It was there that she told me it was over. That was the moment when I felt the deepest cut ever. Bigger that the absence of my father, more powerful than the blows of a mother attempting to instill discipline; in my ears, it was even louder than the helicopters and machine-gun fire of the military. Unrequited love was almost the death of me.

That night, I went to a gas station near my home and purchased thirty tablets of Tylenol. The thought of living without love was worse than living at all in my eyes. I took them. But before lying down for what I thought was going to be my last sleep, I called my mother, who had already lost her brother to suicide earlier that year. I told her what I had done, and my hysteria was matched by her thirty-plus years as a nurse. She told me to stick my finger down my throat and meet her at the hospital. I did not make it to heaven that night, but I did meet an angel.

I arrived at my neighborhood's psychiatric ward a while later, filled with hopelessness and despair. How could I go on with life? I thought. It was then that a nurse with a ward full of people with illnesses far more emergent than mine gave me a tour of what her facility looked like, sharing stories of the patients she had under supervision that night. "You don't belong here," she said, in a voice that was both soothing and stern. She ended up giving me a journal, with the instruction to trade my pills for a pen. With that pen, I released my most prized possession—my heart. Three years and three books later, that heart wrote out what has been my most beautiful masterpiece to date: *Dear Woman*, a letter to women all over the world who also know pain, and hurt, and despair. May these words lead you when you feel you can no longer lead yourself.

"In the Beginning..."

"From the moment she was born, the one title that could never be taken away from her was 'Woman.' It would be her first gift from the world and also her largest cross to bear."

E very time a child is born, it is a gift. It is a sign that God has not given up on the world, a sign that life must and most certainly will continue. When God decides to make that child a woman, the gift becomes even more special— special because women at their core are the guardians of our existence, the facilitators of life, and the rawest example of pure, unmanufactured, unadulterated beauty that we have the pleasure of encountering in the entire universe. As deep as that may sound, it is most certainly a true statement.

This beauty is displayed in many different ways. From a woman's shape, to the way she feels, her physical features, her mental capacity, and most certainly her emotional superiority. A woman is the world's most prized possession and must be treated as such. While this is a job that can only be achieved by women accepting and perpetuating the challenge—and men acknowledging it, the foundation must be laid from within.

> *"It is imperative that all women understand that no one, man or woman, can accurately love you until you love yourself first, and more importantly, love yourself most."*

Being a woman is an opportunity to be fearless and feminine, brave and beautiful, strong and sensitive. All at once. As a woman, you have the power to be both the target and the missile in almost any situation or environment.

We live in a world that puts women first and last. Historically, men have always treated women as their subordinates. The irony here is that the lion's share of decisions men make, both long range and day-to-day, are in some way, shape, or form, whether subconsciously or knowingly, for women. The million-dollar question is, why? I'll get to that. For now, understand this:

Whether it be for their mother, the woman they desire, the woman who is their partner, or the woman they bring into the world themselves—the cars men drive, the clothes men wear, a man's physical appearance, desire for social status, and just about anything else a man does are almost all done to impress some woman. That's not up for debate. This gives a woman the opportunity to achieve the upper hand in almost any situation where her femininity is matched by a male presence.

But women, please note: with great power comes great responsibility; responsibility to yourself, responsibility to the world, responsibility to *your* world—and everything you let in it. This includes a responsibility for you to protect yourself from anything that threatens your happiness, challenges your womanhood, or attempts to make you feel like you have to be someone different than who you are. **Period.**

Dear Woman,

Before you were anything,
you were a woman.
Before friend...
Before lover...
Before girlfriend, partner, wife, or other...
You were woman.
Let no title,
whether it be manufactured by society
to define your existence in the world,
allow you to change whom you permit in your world.
The title of "woman" came before,
will never change during,
and most certainly will remain after.
You must never lose that title while in search for
or trying to maintain any other.
"Woman" is the crown.
The titles are merely jewels.

"The Crown..."

"In a perfect world, a woman receives her crown from her father, and her mother shows her how it is to be worn."

As a woman grows, she becomes more exposed to the world: to its rawness, its realness, its beauty, its pain. Along the way, she learns how to be a woman in that world. In a perfect world, this is done at home by watching her mother and father work together and seeing how they raise their young woman and letting the love they have for each other set the example for how she is to be treated.

In a perfect world, how a woman learns to be a woman is by first observing how her father treats her mother. This is followed by how her mother reacts and then reciprocates, returning that love, attention, respect, and admiration to him. If done correctly, a young woman will get a bird's-eye view of what love means and what respect looks like, and she will have most of the necessary tools to prepare her for the real world.

Sounds good, right? The truth of the matter is that sometimes our world is not so perfect. Many of us live in what society calls "broken" homes. I am not a fan of labeling these homes as broken, because whether we realize it or not, sometimes our minds subconsciously accept these terms in a negative way. Sometimes such descriptions may cause us to feel guilt or shame about our family structure. While some young women may be wise enough to understand, some may not. Even if one child develops insecurity or self-worth issues because of a label she had nothing to do with creating, we have a problem.

"The last thing you want for a child, especially a woman child, is for her to begin life believing that she is broken or that she is a product of something that was broken, especially when the break happened well before her arrival."

Since we're not using broken, I would argue to call these situations alternative homes. Nonetheless, many a woman has not had, does not have, and unfortunately will not have the opportunity to witness both of her parents in the home, laying the foundation for how she is to act and be treated. There are many reasons why this often doesn't happen. It could be anything from death and divorce to a change of heart. In any event, the person who hurts most is the child. My heart goes out to each and every one of you.

If no one else has yet, let me apologize on behalf of those responsible for you falling victim to this unfortunate circumstance. Furthermore, I'm here to tell you that while it is indeed unfortunate, there is a light at the end of the tunnel. In fact, there is light *in* the tunnel.

1. **Understand that it is not your fault.** The same way having children doesn't bring families together, it doesn't tear them apart either. No matter what you think or how you feel, if your parents' relationship did not work, it was because of them—not you.

2. **You are not alone!** While your path to the crown is not ideal, it is most certainly still possible to achieve, and your situation is actually pretty common. The solution is that you may just have to give yourself your own crown— and teach yourself how to wear it. Hey, look on the bright side, at least you'll know it fits!

3. **There is a lesson in even the saddest of situations.** Nobody else can set a better standard for how you can be treated than you. As much as you can learn by watching a family that did work, you can learn by being a part of one that didn't.

Hopefully you feel a little better about yourself, but you're still not done. Actually, you're just beginning. So, what is to be done? First, be thankful, thankful for what you do have and who you have it with—whether it's a mother, father, grandparent, guardian, older sibling, or perhaps at times even a complete stranger. Regardless of how much better you think they could have been to you or how much of a more "comfortable" lifestyle you think you could have had, there are 400,000 children in foster care or up for adoption right now because someone decided that they weren't even worth trying to raise.

As a woman, you have to understand that this world is not fair and that no one in it owes you anything, not even your parents. As you grow into womanhood, you'll learn that the people who have titles in your life are sometimes the ones who hurt you the most. You'll also learn that not everybody who's supposed to care does. So, what do you do with that? You can either let it break you or let it make you. The choice is yours.

Now about that crown...want to know a secret? It's already there. It's just waiting for you to put it on. It's waiting for you to look in the mirror and say, "My home may have been 'broken,' but I am whole." It's waiting for you to say that you can't change your past, but you're ready to take full responsibility for your future. I think we would all love to have witnessed real love at home as children. Of course, it's a beautiful thing to be brought up in an environment where you get to see people in love firsthand, all day, every day. When it's done correctly, it's obvious that it makes you want to duplicate it in your own family in the future. However, sometimes it doesn't work like that.

Sometimes you'll learn how to wear your crown by watching how your mother doesn't always wear hers. Sometimes you'll discover how you want to be treated by witnessing how your mother is mistreated. You'll see how important it is to find somebody who wants a family before you two start doing things that make families, since you'll have witnessed how hard it was on your mother doing it alone. You might be in a situation where your father is the one giving you your crown and telling you how to wear it. It might be a situation where your mother isn't even able to give you yours because she's still waiting for someone to give her hers.

There might be other things going on within your family that I haven't mentioned here. Every woman's situation is different, and no woman's situation is perfect. So, this is what you do, you work

harder. You take it upon yourself to accept what you cannot change
and use it as fuel to make it anyway. You take a hard look at what
was wrong with your family life and where your parents fell short
and use it. Not being able to witness the crown at home is not a
handicap unless you make it one. At the end of the day, regardless
of where you were raised, who you were raised by, and who
stood around watching you and chose not to help, you have the
responsibility to yourself, above anyone or anything else, to be the
best woman you can possibly be.

You have a duty to go and get your crown, place it on your own
head, and keep moving. It's the only way. Otherwise, you're going
to sell yourself short. You're going to start questioning your worth
because no ever told you that you were priceless. You're going
to start giving people discounts because part of you will feel like
you've been alone your entire life. So, the first chance you get,
you'll let someone in, not realizing that some men may not be
interested in you because they see your crown, but they will be
interested because they see that you don't have one.

Go and get your crown.

*The more she found **herself**, the less she felt the **need** to find a man that made her feel like she was **worthy**.*

*A man's job is not to **give** a woman her crown.*

*It is only their job to **respect** it.*

"Setting the Table..."

*"A woman's first line of defense is her standards.
They are the bar by which she differentiates who is
even worth her time. How will you ever know how
much work a person is willing to put in if you don't
require any in the first place?"*

L et's face it, no matter how low you set your standards, no matter how much you're willing to compromise, there are always going to be people who feel like it is still too much work. It will have you questioning everything about yourself and almost nothing about them. You will start second-guessing everything that you thought you had figured out—from what you require to what you will and will not accept. This is a mistake.

"Love is an unfiltered ocean. Your standards are like the purifier that you use to weed out the things that can be harmful to you. The smaller the holes, or the more detailed you are about the standards you have, the more contaminants you remove and the more people you can eliminate."

There are different levels to finding yourself, one of which is finding people that complement you. This is sometimes seen as the hardest of all levels because it usually takes the longest, and sometimes we feel as if this is the level we have the least control over. The key is to not dwell on it so much. Many people look at this level like it's some sort of competition. It isn't. Some people feel that if they don't have a line around the corner of candidates waiting to take a seat at their table, then somehow there must be something wrong with their product or establishment. This is not always true. Sometimes people draw crowds because of popularity, which isn't always good. Sometimes people draw crowds because they are giving something away. This is even worse.

It's not about how many people want to wait in line, or how many people are interested in sitting down at the table with you. It's about you. It's about who you open your doors to; it's about who you feel comfortable enough sitting down at the table with; it's about who you are willing to feed, with your time, energy, attention, and love. You will make out better in the long run. I promise you. The saying, "Quality over Quantity," applies so much here. Do you want to be seen as a fast-food chain or a five-star restaurant? Truth be told, it all depends on how you feel about the product you are serving.

The first thing you must focus on doing is setting the table. Setting your table can be as simple as making it perfectly clear to whomever desires a seat what is on the menu and what is not. The clearer you make this in the beginning, the fewer problems you'll have in the end. Where a lot of people go wrong is offering people things that aren't necessarily on their menu. If this happens, you'll find yourself bending over backwards trying to please people in ways that you aren't comfortable with. Pretty soon you'll get tired of doing that. Then who do you blame? Be careful what you offer. Set your table, and make sure the menu is in ink, not pencil.

Keep in mind that you must be fair and firm. Fair, because when you set the table, the standard of the person you require should be equal to the type of service they receive. You can't expect a man to wear a suit jacket to a restaurant where the hostess is wearing jeans and a T-shirt, right? So, make sure you embody the same standards you require.

As far as firm goes, this is where a lot of people go wrong. A lot of times, we meet someone, and they're close. Other times, we just think they're close. Know the difference. Remember, it's one thing to have a bar that bends, but it's completely different to have one that moves up and down. If you set your table and develop your list of things you won't tolerate, cool. Then you have to compose another list which allows you to decide who's even worthy of sitting down at your table. Now you're in good shape; don't mess that up. Next, and most importantly, watch out for those who slip through the cracks. That's when you need to pull out the *firm*. The firm is what's going to stop you from falling for the "best so far" or the "first decent one in a while." While this might seem like a short-term victory, ultimately you could be making a long-term mistake.

Set your table and stick to it.

DEAR WOMAN,

Sometimes,
you'll just be too much woman.
Too smart.
Too beautiful.
Too strong.
Too much of something
that makes a man feel like less of a man,
which will start making you feel
like you have to be less of a woman.
The biggest mistake you can make
is removing jewels from your crown
to make it easier for a man to carry.
When this happens, I need you to understand:
You do not need a smaller crown—
You need a man with bigger hands.

"The skin you're in..."

"One of the most beautiful things to witness is observing a woman who has fallen in love with herself; one who accepts her flaws and appreciates her gifts, but is most proud of how well the two fit together."

I cannot stress enough the importance of self-love. Once you find it, it will truly be your best friend. It's the key to living a positive life. It's about acceptance, it's about honesty, and it's about being content. It's about loving who you see in the mirror, whether it's 6 a.m. on a Tuesday in your bathroom or 10 p.m. in the mirror of your car on a Saturday night. They are the same woman.

Many women get too caught up in what society thinks is beautiful. It's ok to see beauty in others and appreciate it, but what you should never do is see the beauty in someone else and let it make you feel uncomfortable about you.

"Everybody wants to be the girl in the magazine, but the girl in the magazine isn't even the girl in the magazine."

When you don't have that self-love, you go looking for it. You start second-guessing yourself when it comes to your beauty. You'll start wondering how you can make yourself beautiful. Be careful.

Ask yourself, "How far am I willing to go?" There is a difference between playing with makeup and wanting a new face, or between wanting to lose a few pounds and not eating today because the way someone else looked yesterday makes you want to look like her tomorrow. Instead, give credit where credit is due, including to yourself. You are a model, too. It's just that the magazine you should be on the cover of hasn't gone to print yet. They haven't written the song yet for the music video you're supposed to star in. So, should that stop you? Absolutely not, not when the whole world is your runway. There isn't a height, weight, skin tone, hairstyle, or "look" that's trending. You know what's really in and never going out of style? You. The sooner you realize it, the sooner you'll crack a smile when you see those people who try too hard to be someone else —the people who spend hours getting ready to be seen for minutes. Don't let that be you. Life is lived by the second. Don't waste it trying to get ready for the world. Wake up, look in the mirror, and ask yourself, "Is the world ready for me?" Love the skin you're in—if not, you're going to wake up one day and not even recognize yourself.

DEAR WOMAN,

Never forget that you're beautiful.
When the makeup can't seem to beat your face enough.
When the corsets and body wraps
can't shrink your waist enough.
Be woman enough
to look yourself in the mirror and say,
"This is my body, and I love it just the way it is."
Be your own woman crush,
no matter what day it is.
Whether you're constantly in designer clothes,
or constantly having real life situations
that take the part of your check you had planned
to use to buy your clothes.
Remember, it isn't what you wear,
or how you wear it—
it's about not letting what's on your body affect your spirit.
When you can't fill out a two-piece the way you want to,
remember, God is your plastic surgeon.
If He wanted you to have it,
He would have given it to you.

"Daddy..."

"Naturally, a woman's first love should be her father. However, when it's not, it's not."

To the women who grew up with one: To say that there isn't some sort of supernatural connection that happens between a father and his daughter throughout the process of raising her is difficult to do. A good dad makes moms jealous, boyfriends nervous, and the world just a little bit easier to handle. There are so many women who will testify that their father was the first man they ever fell in love with. There are women who will swear that the love, attention, support and encouragement they received from Dad, and sometimes even the lack of it, were probably the single most important aspects of their growth.

A woman who has that type of connection with her father no doubt has and/or will have an easier transition into becoming a woman. To those women, I want you to take a moment to realize how fortunate you are. If he's around, shoot him a text, tell him, "Thank you." Everybody likes to feel appreciated, even Dad. From the hugs and kisses to the walks and talks, from the screaming and yelling to the embarrassing phone calls and strict rules, everything was done for a reason. No matter what, he was always that lap to sit on, a shoulder to cry on, and that extra twenty bucks when you needed it. Cherish those memories.

Appreciate the good times as well as the tough ones. Having a dad is a beautiful thing, even when some of the decisions he makes or some of his actions as your dad aren't so beautiful. Understand that as with life, there is no handbook that comes with fatherhood. There is no bonus you get in your paycheck every week or discount card you receive in the mail for raising a child. The only real incentive you get is maybe a cool card and a free meal on Father's Day or a couple extra gifts with your name under the Christmas tree, and that maybe twenty-five years from now, your daughter might call you to say, "Thank you." He may fall short, but those are just the places where you can stand tall. He may not say he's proud of you, so be proud of yourself. Be grateful for it all, because the only bad father is the one who doesn't try.

To the women who had to grow up without one: I know what it's like to feel empty—to feel like there is a void in your life, like something is missing. I also know that there aren't too many words I can say that can replace not having a father. My only advice is, "You can't miss what wasn't there." I need you to understand that being a father is just a choice, a choice that you make to be man enough to take care of your responsibilities. This is a decision that every man must make on his own. They'll either do it or they won't. The problem with choices is sometimes people don't always make the right ones. But that isn't your fault. Some dads go above and beyond, some do the best that they can, and some don't do much at all. It's unfortunate, but there isn't a law to make men be fathers, no matter how badly some young women need one.

I know it's tough. Sometimes you don't think about it. Sometimes you think about it until it hurts. Those are feelings that you're allowed to feel, so by all means, cry if you want to cry, or get angry for a second and throw a temper tantrum. That is totally fine. Anything after that, and you've given the thought too much attention. In some cases, you've just given thirty seconds more to your situation than your father ever will. That is too much time to waste on someone who doesn't matter. No, it's not wrong to say they don't matter, and they don't matter now because you didn't matter then. Just don't sit there and act like the universe had it out for you or the "Dad Fairy" didn't decide to leave a father under a pillow. It didn't go down like that.

As much as being a father is an honor and a privilege, as much as it's probably the one thing where as a man, all we have to do is try in order to be loved and appreciated, it's also an option, one that some men just aren't ready for.

This is not your battle to fight. You must continue to be the woman you were destined to be in spite of all the hurdles life throws in your way, including this one. The most important thing is to remember that what doesn't break you makes you stronger. This will be just another test that you turn into a testament of how you made it regardless. It will show you a woman can be a woman without a man's help. Use the pain for a purpose. If the time ever comes when you two meet again, have as much forgiveness in your heart as you do pain. Understand that while he might have been able to be in your life sooner, if he had been, you wouldn't be the woman you are today.

Dear Woman,

Life comes in threes:
Who gave you life. Who you bring into this life. And you.
The first two are usually the most talked about.
Maybe it's because they usually last the longest,
or maybe it's because society makes you think
that your life isn't valid
unless you're giving it to someone else.
Too many women spend too much
of their lives at a bus stop,
at the corner of the block where they grew up,
with everything they own,
everything they've learned,
crammed in three suitcases,
a book bag, and a cardboard box
with "fragile" written on every side.
Waiting.
Waiting to be picked up and taken away
by a knight in shining armor, like a damsel in distress,
like the last five-year-old to be picked up from school.
It's time to get you off that corner.
If you can't go home, go somewhere else,
and make it home.
Sit on your couch with your favorite book,
a glass of wine, and a candle.
Unbothered.
What good is giving your life to someone else,
if you haven't even given it to yourself?

"Third Part of Life..."

"If you're engaged, turn the page."

How old do you want to be when you get married? Twenty-eight, thirty, thirty-three? Yesterday? Why? Because somebody told you that's what you're "supposed" to do at that age? I'm telling you right now, don't fall for it! Yes, marriage is cool, but you know what else sounds cool? Living your damn life. I know some people mature faster than others, and sometimes life puts us in situations where we need to do what's best for our situations, not ourselves. So, if you've got one of those high school sweethearts that never turned sour, I get that. If you get pregnant (please, be careful) and you decide that it's in the best interest of the child for the two of you to start a family, think about it again, and if you do decide to go through with it, I get that.

Right now, I'm talking to the woman who's tired of getting wedding invitations and having to buy new dresses to go watch other women commit the rest of their lives to somebody. I'm talking to the woman who wants to hop on the next man with a nice smile and half a brain and ride him into the sunset of "marriage" because you're tired of trying to find a guy who can text you back in a decent amount of time when you're talking about something other than hooking up. This is for you.

Before you think about giving the rest of your life to someone else, ask yourself a couple questions. How many years have you given to you? How many years have you worked for yourself, on yourself, by yourself, with yourself? Let's do some quick math here: As a woman, you spend roughly the first seventeen to eighteen years working for your parent(s), right? Everything including "wash this, clean that, move that, bring me this, don't do that, be home at this time, you can't wear that, you can't go there, who is this and why are they at my door step," plus a whole bunch of other rules, right?

Then your eighteenth birthday comes along and you are finally free —well, sort of. Many of you will go to college; some will enter the work force, and some will do a little of both. Either way, you're going to finally begin to start making some of your own decisions and living your own life. Keep going.

These next few years, from eighteen to twenty-five, are crucial. This is when you start becoming your own woman. You'll start figuring out what you like, what you don't, who you like, and who you don't. The good thing is, you're well on your way. The not so good thing is your life isn't really all yours yet. In college, you might not have your parents breathing down your neck, but college life isn't a joke. You'll have papers to write, homework to do, and parties to crash (not too many, though), and will probably be the most dating freedom you've had your whole life, especially if you had one of those moms that just had to meet every guy that wanted to take you to the movies or the dad who asks twenty-one questions to guys that even you don't know the answers to yet. College is your first taste of freedom. Enjoy it.

If you decide to go straight into working from high school, your focus should be on saving up enough money to move as far away from your parents' house as you can, but close enough to still be able to sleep in your old room if the weather is going to be bad or if you're out of food. You'll realize that you were probably better off staying there a little longer, because leaving the lights on all the time isn't a big deal until YOU are the one paying the electric bill.

Once you're out, enjoy it! This is your first taste of a little freedom; don't let it go to your head or your heart. If you've just moved out of your parents' house, don't let only forty-five minutes go by until all of a sudden, you're moving someone into yours. Your focus should be on your career, because either you're at an entry level in your job or just getting started in your own business—either way, you're in competition with people who are much older than you and much more experienced than you, and you have a lot to learn about yourself and your business. There aren't enough hours in a day to be a student of school, a student of life, and a student of love all at the same time. You're well on your way though, don't stop now. Keep going.

> *"Your teenage years and early twenties should be
> dedicated to you figuring out how the world works,
> not you trying to give the world to someone else."*

Twenty-five to thirty. Okay, so if you're on track, these should be some of the best years of your life. The only aisle you should be worrying about walking down is the one that has your diploma at the other end. You worked so hard these last four to six years. (Some people think college is so dope that they decide to stick around a little longer. No judgment here.)

Now it's time to enjoy the fruits of your labor and GET A JOB. (I'm just trying to warn you before your parents do.) This is when life starts to get a little easier—though not easy enough for you to think you can find a good job and a good man the week after graduation. It might be easier like, "I can get a job that pays me enough money to afford my rent, eating, and shopping—all with the same check…and still have money for gas." (lol, but seriously) If you've been a working woman these last couple of years, let this be the time that you take working on your life and career to another level. It's time to get a raise; it's time to get a promotion; it's time to apply for a different position, maybe even a new job. There are so many ways you can grow that have nothing to do with love. Try a few of them.

At the end of the day, this is just a guide…a couple of suggestions from a man who's watched so many women put so much pressure on a situation that really requires so little. For seventeen to eighteen years, you belong to your parents, and then you belong to either your college or the early stage of your career. The last thing you want to do is belong to someone else for the next sixty years before you even belong to yourself. Don't be so used to making other people happy that you forget the most important person in the crazy roller-coaster ride called life: you.

There are some women who will meet great people early in life—people who will be just as confused as you are—and you two are going to figure it out together. Along the way, you two might realize that you don't want to figure it out alone or with other people, and that will be a beautiful thing. That is organic love. That is best-friend love. It is not to be confused with settling. Others, though, will get caught up about where their life is. They will have the mother who keeps reminding them, "You're not getting any younger," and somehow, no matter how the conversation starts, "grandkids" always come up. Eventually, these women will start second-guessing where they are in life. Don't let that be you. What messes some people up is the idea in their head of where they are supposed to be in life. There are three parts to it: living with your parents, living with your partner, and living with you.

Make sure you get your fair share of all three.

DEAR WOMAN,

There are two souls inside of you.
One Mother. One Wife.
Both givers. Both protectors.
Both dying to be set free.
The problem is,
you'll notice that they both
usually appear around the same time.
And you'll notice some men you meet
will need one just as badly as they need the other.
Please, be careful
which one you bring into your relationship.
If you don't learn how to separate the two,
you will treat your man like your son.
The wife in you will make love to him,
while the mother will allow him
to do no wrong in your eyes.
The wife in you will accept him for who he is,
while the mother in you will try to raise him
like he is your own.
The problem is,
when you teach a boy how to be a man—
if you do it right,
he isn't supposed to come home.

"two"

"If you have to be both, be neither."

Sometimes, being a woman can be a gift and a curse, especially when you begin to feel everything so deeply. As you grow as a woman, you'll notice that you begin to react to people and situations with a certain attitude. It will become almost second nature. All the emotion and compassion that a woman naturally possesses will manifest itself in her everyday life. You have to learn how to manage those feelings or you will find yourself in a place where far too many women end up. They start being mothers to their boyfriends. It might sound like a stretch, but really, it's not. It's honestly the result of just a couple of common occurrences that, when combined, can create the "perfect storm" that might get you knee-deep into a situation where you are using these gifts the wrong way.

The first soul is "mother." Some women get it from their mother; some women learn it by being a mother to themselves. In any event, this is the soul that makes you want to be a protector, a forgiver, a nurturer, and a fixer. What's wrong with that? Nothing. It's a necessary list of traits that every woman should have which will be useful to her in the future when she must be those things to her own child. Remember, the key word here is CHILD. The second soul is "wife." This, too, can be learned by a young woman who watched how her mother treated whoever the male figure in her household was. This, too, isn't a bad thing. In fact, when it's done right, every young woman who witnesses it in her home will want to have it for themselves after having seen how valuable this soul was to her mother's happiness. If a young woman doesn't witness it there, she will definitely do so in the world.

"Marriage and love are everywhere. They have a way of making you feel like there is this big party going on and that you're missing out on it. There might be, but it's definitely one where you want to get an invitation to it instead of crashing it."

Witnessing these two souls, mother and wife, at first hand definitely does help; more importantly, though, you must be able to know when and where to use them. This plays a role in how you operate with these souls. The problem isn't that you have them, it's knowing how to separate the two, and it's finding a man who doesn't need you to be both. Some people might say that the similarities between mother and wife are pretty significant. They are. They share a lot of the same characteristics, but they are two totally different things.

There are some men out here who need a mother more than they need a wife. They need to be taken care of in ways that are beyond what you should be willing to offer. Don't get so caught up in desiring to be a wife to a man that you start being a mother to him first. Subconsciously, this is your way of trying to prepare him for you. This is a mistake. If you do this, you begin to nurture him while trying to fall in love with him at the same time. It's going to be difficult to recognize because, like I said, the two souls run so closely together. You'll notice that you're in trouble when the only time you feel like a wife is in the bedroom. Any other time, you find yourself being the mother. You'll do more cleaning than getting cleaned up to go out on a date. You'll do more teaching than learning. You'll be more excited about the man he has the potential to be than the man that you have. Before you know it, you'll have raised him. Be careful.

If you're not, you might just raise a boy to be a better man for another woman.

DEAR WOMAN,

There are a few things that are worse than murder,
like a woman who ends up becoming
just like the man who hurt her.
Sometimes worse.
These days, half the time,
you act like you don't even have a heart.
The other half is:
"I've got one, but I don't even know if it still works."
It's probably because you don't even know
whether you love him or hate him yet.
The only thing you're 100 percent sure of is that it still hurts.
So, now, you're running around, acting like the girl version
of him
when you need to be finding the version of you that sticks
around after it doesn't work out with some of these men.
It's sad that he left.
It's worse that, ever since he did,
you haven't even been close to right.
So, now, instead of looking for love,
you're content with bringing just anybody to your home
at night.
It's ironic how the one thing you hold onto after he's gone
is the one thing you wish he'd never brought with him.
It's bad enough that he stole your light.
It's even worse that you ran in the dark with him.

"For Better or Worse"

"Every man that enters and exits a woman's life changes her in some way. The only question is, how?"

I t starts in the beginning. Most of the time, when a woman decides to deal with a man she has some concerns about before she gives her heart to him, she's usually right. A woman's intuition is her best friend. The sad part is that, sometimes, the reasons why a woman shouldn't deal with a specific man are the same reasons why she ends up going through with it anyway. I don't know whether it has something to do with the saying about how "Every woman wants a bad guy who will be good to her" or the one that goes, "Why do good girls like bad guys?" Both are ridiculous.

"There is a difference between trying to change a bad guy and letting a bad guy change you."

What I need you to understand is every person you let into your life changes you. It is up to you if it's going to be for better or for worse. Whether you let them in for a half a second, half a year, or half your life, they all rub off on you. This is why I can't stress enough that you must keep positive people around you. When you have a bunch of good people in your corner, it helps you to recognize the bad ones, because they will stand out. It's like if you have a bunch of apples in a basket; if most of them are fresh, you will notice the rotten one quickly. It is not enough to just notice it, though, you must also remove it. If you don't, that bad apple might destroy the whole bunch, or it might destroy you.

Some people slip through the cracks; either they aren't who you thought they were, or you knew who they were and just didn't think they would be that way with you. It happens in politics; it happens in business; it happens in love. I know it's frustrating when you find out otherwise, but what's worse is when you let it affect you and affect how you live your life after you know. To expect the world to be fair to you, to expect the world to treat you the same way you treat it, is nothing but suicide. There are too many people who just aren't good people. Sometimes, it isn't even their fault, but it is NEVER yours. You can't walk around expecting things to be fair, because they won't be. That's why you are supposed to appreciate the real ones more, since there aren't that many of them walking around. That is only half the battle, though. The second half is dealing with what you let the not-so-real ones do to you. To let the way the world treats you change the way you treat yourself and the way you treat the world afterwards is murder.

I see too many women who deal with guys who break their hearts. If you are one of those women, I don't know whether to blame him for breaking your heart or blame you for giving it to him in the first place, so I will not do either. What I will do, though, is tell you that under no circumstances are you to EVER let what he did to your heart make you act like you don't have one; nor are you to ever, consciously or subconsciously, let it make you run around and break other peoples' hearts. If you were a good person before him, be a good person in spite of him, and continue to be a good person after him. Do you know why?

Whether you realize it or not, no matter how far away he is from you physically, if a bad guy is still in your heart and still in your head, if he is still controlling how you act with yourself or with any other man after him, he is still winning. How can you let a man win when he isn't even playing anymore? Answer: While he is no longer playing you, he is affecting you enough that you're playing yourself.

First, you have to understand that him hurting you had to happen. It had to happen because he wasn't the person for you, and you didn't pick up on the signs. It had to get worse, not so it could get better, but so you could get better. You might have even picked up on the signs, but you thought it was love, so you didn't mind going through the rough patches. Either way, physically he's gone, but he has rubbed off on you. He was bad to you, so instead of you being happy that you got out, you were upset that you got your feelings hurt, so you decided to be bad to the rest of the world. You started saying things like, "If you can't beat 'em, join 'em," and "All guys are the same." Some of you go as far as saying, "I'm going to treat them the way they treat me." Don't do it. Why? Because as soon as you do, what you're saying is that you are going to let the way bad guys treat you dictate how you treat potentially good guys. You're going to attract more bad guys, since they will see themselves in you and feel like it's a match made in heaven because they finally found a woman who thinks and feels the way they do. This might work for a second, but do you know what's going to happen? You're going to spend more time with this new guy, and then you're going to begin forgetting about the old one because you're "happy." Then you're going to start acting like yourself again, only to realize that he liked you for who he thought you were because of what the guy before did to you. When he sees the real you, he might not like you as much because you're not the person he met initially. Then you will be back to square one: emotionally murdered, again. This time, it will be your fault.

For some of you, it won't happen that way. For some of you, what will happen is you will be turned off by love completely. You will flat-out hate men. You will become cold and bitter. You will look at men as objects, and as nothing more than an item to satisfy a specific need. You'll ask yourself what you need from a man and only look for that. Most of the time, it will be material things (like money), sex, attention, or company. Other times, you will seek revenge and try to break other hearts because yours is broken. It's like they say, "Hurt people hurt people." This is worse than murder. This is when you need a reality check.

You can't just walk around hurting people.

Dear Woman,

Boys will be boys.

The good. The bad.

As well as the, "I didn't see that one coming."

More often than not,

you will meet the second two

more often than you'll meet the first.

No worries, everybody makes mistakes.

The good thing is nothing lasts forever;

so, the only bad decisions you have to live with

are the ones you let live with you.

It's kind of like nail polish:

Some colors look good in the display case

but are terrible when they reflect against your skin.

Just like you can't be mad at the bottle, you can't be mad at

the man.

His job was not to be the color you like.

It is your job to figure out

whether or not you like the color he is.

If you ever get to a point

where you are surprised by one's actions,

understand that, every time a man reveals his true colors,

it is an opportunity.

Not to convince yourself that you like the color,

but to have the patience to sit down and try again.

"Colors"

"Sometimes, you don't know where you're going until you get there, but just because you get there, doesn't mean you have to stay there."

Sometimes, you won't know how you really feel about a person until you're with that person. Sometimes, it's because people don't give the best parts of themselves to just anybody. Sometimes, it's because people are good at pretending to be someone else. Some of the pretenders do it because they think being a certain type of person will put them in the best position to get what they want from you. Other times, it's because there are people out here who want to be somebody other than who they are, so when they advertise themselves, they attempt to sell you a house that hasn't even been built yet—in hopes that you're willing to invest in them enough to complete the project.

"In time, everyone reveals who they really are.
Sometimes, it's on the first date; sometimes, it's
the first time you need them to be something else
other than what they had planned on being for
you. That might be when you realize that they
are the one, or that may be the moment when
you realize that you just got robbed. Don't stick
around. Accept it and find the exit."

When you're knee-deep in something, whether it's a business investment, a career, or love, it becomes so hard to cut your losses. It becomes so difficult to accept the fact that you just made a bad decision. I want you to get in the habit of comparing things that are of importance to things that are not so important, if only to cut back on some of the pressure that everyone feels about trying to make things work.

Most women are familiar with getting their nails done and the process that goes along with it. The similarities are actually quite believable. You walk into the nail salon, and it's time to pick your color. Now, you may have an idea of what color you want and why. It might be because you thought it looked nice in the bottle on the shelf, it might be because of how it looked on someone else, or it could be because you had your mind made up that you were going to try something different.

None of these are bad reasons to try a color or a person. Just don't do it because of an outfit; it might be good for a night, but the rest of the month, you're screwed. So, you try it out, and after the paint dries, you stick out your hand and look at it. As it's pressed against your skin, don't be afraid to hate it if it's not what you expected it to be. You might just be a shade off, or purple just might not be your color.

The good thing is, just like nail polish, people are removable. Now, some people may say, "Girl, just let it grow on you." The problem with that is, some people will spend more time with the color and then go back tomorrow and change it. Others will leave it because they are too lazy, too busy, too stingy, or too impatient to reinvest in the process. Don't let that be you.

There are too many colors out there for you to make yourself like a specific one.

DEAR WOMAN,

I think you've just got too much time on your hands.

But instead of you finding a hobby,

you let your emotions and the weather get the best of you.

So, you go out and find you a body.

Somebody. Anybody. Just a body to keep you warm.

Then, when your body gets all hot but your heart's not,

you're just setting yourself up for the storm.

Just because it's raining men doesn't mean

you need to step outside with your mouth open.

You'll catch a cold or a stone-cold creep

before you find one that sees your heart,

if you're running around with your blouse open.

You don't really want a boyfriend as bad as you think you do.

You just miss the text messages letting you know

that there's somebody out there

who likes you enough to think of you.

What I'm going to need from you

is for you to start thinking of yourself more.

There's nothing wrong with buying an extra blanket

and a body pillow and keeping yourself warm.

At least, that way, you know exactly who you're laying

down with.

The last thing you want to do is put on those red shoes and

makeup just to find somebody to be a clown with.

"Responsibility"

"Sometimes, the more assets you have, the more of a liability they become."

Let me be the first to tell you that I know personally what it feels like to be lonely. I also know what it feels like to be desired by many people while being lonely. It's a really tough position to be in. To get through it safely, you've got to learn how to manage these feelings, or else you're going to be doing a whole bunch of nothing. With great beauty, great power, great popularity—shoot—even with a great job and a great apartment, comes great responsibility – a responsibility not to let what you bring to the table, multiplied by the fact that there isn't anybody at your table, make you go out and start having auditions. Why? Because not everybody that is interested is eligible.

"One of the most dangerous combinations around is a good woman with too much time on her hands."

There is no shortage of men. Now, *good* men—we could have a spirited discussion about that, but let's just say that, of course, there are more Hondas than Bentleys out here on the road, as there should be. What makes a car valuable isn't just the price, it's the fact that it is exclusive.

However, guess what? You're exclusive, too. So, you have to learn how to accept your exclusivity, and be woman enough to understand that not everybody can afford a Bentley, but that doesn't mean they won't walk into your dealership dressed up in their favorite outfit with a couple of dollars in their pocket looking for a test drive.

Meanwhile, you, the owner of the dealership, are just dying to let somebody take you around the block. I'm going to need you to be stronger than that. I'm going to need you to be able to turn some people away at the door and down the street. Some people don't even need to know where your dealership is, and it's not because you're stuck up or conceited. Those are things people will say when they realize that it's not a queen's job to explain their crown.

You need to be able to turn people away because time is too valuable to be wasted.

Instead, keep your car clean and ready to go. There is so much more to be doing out here to better yourself. There are so many opportunities that are available to experience life in different ways. Find one or six. Find enough that you'll be so busy you don't even have time to realize. Be so busy working on yourself that you don't even notice no one came in today, this week, or this month—busy enough that someone either has to be really persistent or a really serious candidate for you to fork over those keys.

If not, the alternative is going to be a line around the corner made up of everyone from the CEO to the janitor, all ready and willing to go for a spin. Before you know it, you'll have more than a few miles on that car; you'll start noticing new scratches and dents every time you turn around. Then, you'll have to lower the price. Keep your car parked. You can start it up every now and then, but you can do that all on your own. Just don't be afraid to be by yourself.

Just because your car has two seats, doesn't mean you need two people.

Dear Woman,

Every man you meet will fall into one of two categories:
Either they are the "directions" or the "destination."
Most of them will reveal which one they are.
All you need to do is be patient.
How do you know?
The "directions" will tell you where you are,
where you went wrong, and where you need to go.
Sometimes the directions are right,
sometimes the directions are as wrong
as the person who is giving them to you.
The most important part is that they will make it perfectly
clear
that you don't belong there.
You just have to pay attention.
You just have to be so committed to get to
wherever it is that you think you need to be,
and so tired of being where you are, that you have to
move on.
No matter how long it takes, no matter how far you must go.
Never be scared to get back in your car
and keep on going down that road.
Sometimes, there won't be any signs on the way
or when you get there.
Sometimes, you'll just know.
Once you finally make it home, it's all over.

"Lost"

"A woman without direction is liable to end up anywhere."

Are you familiar with the saying about how everybody in your life comes into it for a reason? Great. It's totally true. More importantly though, as badly as you want to believe that you are responsible for finding that reason and putting these people in a certain position or giving them a specific title in your life, you're not. Sometimes, you are just supposed to sit back and watch where people put themselves.

Let's say you took my advice on the previous page, and now you're knee-deep in living your own life and not worried about a guy. (Finally!) However, now, you're too deep—so deep that you start attracting some pretty good guys. Before, you were telling yourself how busy you are and how you don't have time to date or fall in love or even go to lunch because "you're really into yourself right now," or you "just got out of something crazy" three years ago! So, you don't even know how to begin to even attempt to give your heart to somebody. I get it. It's easier to say "no, thank you" and go home to your empty house with some TV show like *Scandal* on DVR, ice cream, and your pajamas... at least, it's easier until you look up and five years have passed, and you have all the success in the world but nobody to share it with.

Then, one day, you meet a guy and, for some reason, you get this feeling that you don't want to send him to voicemail. You actually reply to his text massages. You might even pick up the phone and call him first. Shocking, I know. Now, through the course of this newfound friendship, you enjoy the fact that on the way home from work, you have someone to talk to instead of listening to the radio or sitting in silence thinking about how depressing your life is and how the rest of the world is living it up. Great! As time goes on, you'll start to see this person more; you'll start opening up to them about things that actually matter, like what you're afraid of, where you want to be in five years, and how messed up your credit is. You know, the stuff that really matters—not like the generic things, the what-is-your-favorite-color, food, and movie routine that some guys drag a woman through.

The good news is, you did it. You finally put your work, career, and yourself to the side and actually made time for someone else.

The bad news is, sometimes you may be so excited about having someone to open up to that you may not even realize that he isn't the one. Here is where the "direction vs. destination" theory comes in.

"Sometimes a man comes into your life not to make it over the wall, but just to knock it down a little, or to prove to you that there's room for one on the other side."

He will be your directions. He will make you understand that maybe your life isn't so busy; maybe you do have time to let someone in. He might not necessarily be the one, but he can prove to you that you are finally ready and willing to receive the one. He's like the gas station on your way to wherever you're going.

Just don't get stuck there.

Remember, you still need to get home.

Dear Woman,

When dealing with a man,
you must find it as easy to open your mouth
as you do your legs.
Only the things that are open
are the things that can be fed.
When I say fed, I'm not talking about in bed.
I'm talking about those 300 suggestions
about how he can be a better boyfriend
that you've got floating around in your head.
The problem is,
they never seem to be talked about during the pillow talk.
So, if you're still complaining about the issues
you had when you first met him,
yet ever since then,
you've only become better at undressing for him
than addressing them,
no matter what, it's still your fault.
Any woman who doesn't lay the foundation
for how she needs to be treated
is a woman who can't be mad if the man
she's been faithful to has cheated.
As a woman,
it is your responsibility to lay the ground work.
If you don't, you'll fall in love
with a man who won't catch you.
Then, you'll see how hard
hitting the ground hurts.

"Progress Report"

"The only lessons that can't be learned are the ones you don't teach."

Have you ever woken up in the morning, rolled over, looked at the man lying next to you, and thought to yourself, "I could be so much happier?" Really? So, why aren't you? I mean, let's think about it. He was good enough to get your phone number, good enough to get your address, good enough for you to open your door, and good enough to let him make his way into your bedroom and between your legs, and good enough to stay the night. Yet you can't even get breakfast in the morning. That's a damn shame.

You know what's even worse? You're so afraid to lose what he does for you physically that you don't even have the heart to open up that pretty little mouth of yours and tell him how to make you happy. Now, it's really none of my business what goes down in that bedroom—that's between you, him, and whoever you pray to at night. (Just make sure somebody has a condom.) All I'm saying is that there shouldn't be too much of anything going on with your mouth, his mouth, or just about anything else on your body if you can wake up in the morning and know in your heart that you're only getting 50% of what you really need to satisfy you.

Now, before you go waking him up out of his sleep because you're angry that he's not making French toast, I need you to ask yourself a couple of questions: Why am I not happy? What do I need to be happy? Is this guy even the guy to do it for me?

Done? Cool. Now, this is when things get tricky—tricky because, depending on what your agreement was with him, the answers might not be a part of the deal. This is what happens when you put the cart before the heart. Now, you've just opened up a whole new can of worms. Don't blame me, blame yourself. I'm not the one who did it; I just turned the lights on. The good news is that you can't lose. Why? You can either tell him to pick up the worms (because I know how some of you ladies are about bugs), or you can pack up the worms yourself and him too, and send him fishing. The bad news is, it really isn't your choice; you've just got to offer them both and let him pick.

"If the man you're with isn't willing to fix what's broken, he doesn't deserve to have what isn't."

So, this is the moment of truth. This is when you figure out whether you have a "rider" or a "roller." You've got to kick out that progress report; you've got to be firm and let him know: This is where we are, this is where we need to be, and this how you can help me get there. It is important that you have these things figured out before you open your mouth (or anything else), because you can't introduce problems without offering solutions. The man in him will say things like, "What, you want to go shopping or something?" or most men's favorite, "Do you want to do it again?" That's only going to prolong the inevitable.

Figure out why you're not happy and what you need to get happy, and own it. Just be prepared to get there alone, because it's hard to get somebody to buy a cow after you've given them the cereal…or something like that.

DEAR WOMAN,

You want it too badly.

Why can't you be by yourself?

I'm not saying forever.

Just long enough for you to finally fall in love with you first.

Long enough that when a boy you like decides

that he can't handle you,

it doesn't leave you hurt.

Long enough for you to be able to look in the mirror,

wipe the tears from your face,

and say, "You know what, it's his loss."

I'm tired of seeing you give your heart to a man,

only to watch him take it with him when he leaves.

If that's not bad enough,

you try to get under somebody else to get over him—

thinking they can give you what you need.

Opening one door doesn't give you closure to another.

The closure comes when your happiness isn't predicated on

your relationship with some fella.

"Go Home"

"When the party's over, where do YOU go?"

The problem with even some of the most amazing love is that, unless it leads you to the altar or you two can somehow be friends after—don't hold your breath—one day it's going to be over. Some women may take it well; others will think their life is now somehow over. They may just want to crawl under a rock somewhere and break out the sad songs, ice cream, love movies, and candles, and cry their pretty little eyes out. Cool.

Others of you will throw temper tantrums and, via Twitter, bash every man on earth except your daddy. Some of you will send rude, malicious, almost ignorant text messages to his phone, talking about how you didn't even like him that much anyway and how you weren't even happy—you were just pretending. Not as cool because, at one time, he was exactly what you wanted, but okay.

The ones I'm worried about are the ones who forty-five minutes after the break up, knowing damn well that just forty-six minutes ago, you had everything from the baby names to wedding ideas planned out in your head, are now taking everybody off the block list, replying to all those direct messages on Instagram, and approving ex-boyfriends from college on Facebook. You are the ones I'm worried about.

"When you don't allow yourself time to heal after you've been hurt, you take the risk of getting reinfected. The first part of healing is always done alone."

You need to go home. Being in love is like a party, a party that is wall-to-wall fun: The DJ is playing all your favorite songs, the champagne is flowing, all of your friends are there, all of your pictures are coming out cute, and the host just gave you a shout-out on the microphone, putting a smile on your face like way back when you were six years old and got an Easy-Bake Oven for your birthday.

Then, just when you were about to stand on the couch, a fight breaks out—there's screaming and yelling everywhere, and the lights come on. Damn. The good thing is, you'll be able to see clearly. Here is your opportunity to see people for who they are. You'll have an attitude, though, because, just like that last bottle of tequila you ordered twenty minutes ago, you'll have a lot of love left on the table. It sucks, I know, but all good things must come to an end. Some people won't accept that. Some people just don't know how to go home. Some people just have to be somewhere because they spent too much time getting ready. They hardly ever go out to begin with, and they were having a pretty good time.

I don't care what they do. However, you—you have to go home. If not, you're going to mess around and get yourself into some trouble because you don't know how to walk away. You're still drunk in love from the last party, and you just can't stand being alone. So, you don't care where it is, who it is, or how long it's been since you've been home, you just want to keep the party going. Bad move, because what you're not doing is probably the most important part of a relationship after it's over: getting back sober.

That's the part when you're able to sit down in peace and quiet to reflect on what just happened. If you don't give yourself that time, all you're really doing is continuing the old party. What you're forgetting is how you didn't get dressed for this party, you didn't plan for this party, and you might not have even been invited. You just didn't want to waste an outfit. I need you to think with your head here, sweetheart. What man is going to turn you away looking as good as you do when you show up at their door? None. That doesn't mean you need to go inside. What's going to happen is you're going to go in, and you won't know what you're walking into. It might satisfy you for a second, maybe even an hour or two, but ultimately, you'll snap back into reality. When you do, you'll realize that you don't belong there.

DEAR WOMAN,

Sometimes you have to be your own cheerleader.

Some people may want to see you grow,

until your potential is bigger than the box they put you in.

Until the light from your candle shines so brightly

that it blinds them.

They don't know whether to put glasses on

or to blow you out.

Some people will never be happy FOR you

until they are happy WITH themselves.

Have you ever met a person who wants the best for you,

until the best for you

means getting off their boat, so you can walk on water?

Some people don't have the heart to tell you

that you've become too much for them.

So, they try to tell you that your dream is too big.

Really, they're afraid that, one day, reality will set in.

They know the real nightmare is you realizing that the same

people who are supposed to be holding you down

are the ones holding you back.

"Poison"

---

*"Depending on who you share your dreams with,
the nightmare could be them not wanting to be
your reality."*

There was this one couple I came across about two years ago, Chris and Sarah, a guy and a girl who, at one time, were madly in love with each other. They were best friends; they were lovers; they were everything in between. The only real problem was that they were both broke. Normally, that wouldn't be a real problem, because most of us are relatively broke anyway. A few of us make more, but we often spend more, so when it comes down to it, most of us could be doing a lot more for ourselves. We could be doing a lot better financially, but many of us get to a point where we get comfortable. That's a conversation for another time. Back to this couple.

While they were both scratching and surviving together, they were probably the happiest they had ever been or ever would be. When they met, they were both just out of college with nothing but student loans and a degree. They dated for about seven months. They saw each other six days a week, had five-hour conversations on the phone, and lived four blocks away from each other, so they never spent more than three nights in separate beds until the two of them decided to get one place to call their own. It was the sweetest thing. They made lunch out of leftovers, miracles out of paychecks, and love almost every morning. The best part of waking up besides waking up itself is doing it next to someone you love.

Their lives went on this way for about three years. Things weren't perfect, but they had each other. Some days, they had enough for trips to the mall, dinners, drinks, a dozen roses, and the five for $26.50 from Victoria's Secret when they arrived back home. Other days, all they had was each other. No matter what day you asked them, each other was all they ever really needed.

Chris was the manager at his local supermarket. He had started as a cashier there while working through college. After he got his degree in business, he couldn't find a job, so he went back there to be a cashier until he found something permanent. The only thing he found was that, after he had spent the last four years of his life getting a degree, after student loans and credit cards, he was making just about as much as he had before he went to school. Six months later, his supermarket opened another store on the other side of town, and they promoted him because it was cheaper than bringing somebody else on. Sarah had been a fashion major who had dreamed of being a celebrity stylist, but the reality was that she was the head window dresser at Forever 21 in the mall near her college. Sarah loved her job because she got to do what she loved, even though she wasn't doing it for anyone famous.

Sarah had come up in the church. No matter where she was during the week, she would always find herself in the front row of her grandmother's Southern Baptist Tabernacle—every Sunday from 10 o'clock in the morning until whenever they decided to send everyone home. She participated in everything, from the Sunday school to singing in the choir. As she got older, she could never stop singing. While she was at work, she had her McDonald's drive-thru style store headpiece in one ear, chatting with all her coworkers who didn't do anything but talk about everyone who came in and out of the store, from the cute guys to girls they had hated when they were in high school, as well as the brave souls who would end up going to jail because they came out of the dressing room with fewer clothing items than they'd had going in. In the other ear, she had her music. She spent most of her shift retagging and applying sensors to the returns, refolding T-shirts, and of course, dressing the mannequins. She would listen to everything from Vivian Greene to Yolanda Adams. Sometimes, when a good song came on, she would sing just a little bit louder than under her breath. She tried to keep it in as best she could, but sometimes she just couldn't help it.

One Saturday afternoon, she was back in the window dressing the mannequins with the new fall line because it was the only time she could ever use her degree, doing what she loved more than the job itself. That day, her life changed drastically. A song by Keisha Cole called "Love" began playing on her Pandora feed, and if you didn't know any better, you would've thought that Keisha herself was right there in that window.

At about the same time as the chorus came on for the last time, an older lady came walking into the store, looking for a black cami and some leggings. As soon as she set foot inside, before she could even open her mouth to ask where she could find what she needed, she heard Sarah's voice bouncing off the glass window like it was a game-winning three-pointer from half court. She ran over to Sarah and asked her, "Why are you here?" Sarah responded, "My coworker called off work today, and I can use the overtime." The lady began to laugh as she reached into her purse and pulled out her business card. She said, "Your voice is too special for you to be singing to mannequins. If you ever want to do something else besides work overtime with your extra time, give me a call."

The card read, *Regina Phillips, A&R Virgin Records.* Sarah, who was happy with the way her life was going at the time, politely stuck the card in her back pocket, said thank you, and finished the mannequins. On her way home, she thought about the offer. She couldn't wait to get home to tell Chris about what happened today, anticipating that they would laugh about it over spaghetti and meatballs for the fifth time this month.

When Sarah got home, she noticed Chris was in a bad mood. The new store the supermarket had opened wasn't doing well, and his hours were being cut because they had other managers with more seniority. She noticed his sadness so, just as she was about to pull out the card, she jammed it down in her back pocket and started dinner. After eating dinner and watching *Love and Hip Hop*, Sarah did the dishes while Chris was in the bedroom preparing to do the laundry. He wanted to make sure they had enough clean clothes for the week. Last time Chris had done the laundry, he had forgotten to take a pen out of his shirt pocket before putting it in the washer, and it had messed up her favorite sweater. This time, before starting the load, he checked every pocket—shirt and pants—every sock, and he even checked the bottom of the washing machine to make sure the pen from last time wasn't still there. It wasn't, but he did find Regina's card.

Chris started the load, then walked into the kitchen and asked who Regina was. Sarah brushed it off, saying, "Oh, she was just a lady that I met in Forever today who heard me singing." Chris inquired, "Was that it?" Sarah replied, "No, she told me I should give her a call if I wanted to sing." Chris asked her if she wanted to. Sarah said she had never really thought about it until the ride home on the bus today. Chris told her she should give Regina a call. Sarah's face lit up like a Christmas tree, and she replied, "Really?" Chris shrugged and said, "Why not? I already knew you had a gift; we might as well show the world, too."

As the weeks passed, soon there was no more overtime for Sarah. She reallocated most of her free time and even gave up a couple of shifts at work every other week, just so she could meet with Regina and they could write songs and sing hooks as they worked to put together enough music to create an EP. Chris was fine with it; he supported Sarah every chance he got. He would join her at the studio sometimes and bring her dinner if she was coming straight from work. If it was really late, he would travel halfway across town and catch the subway home with her because he didn't want her out that late alone. He was supportive to her the entire time and never complained.

A couple of months passed. Sarah was still both working her day job and working with Regina; they were one song away from completing the project. She would be in the studio until after midnight some nights and would get a ride home from Regina because Sarah only lived a couple exits past her on the freeway. One night, she came home and dinner wasn't made, the house was a mess, and Chris was asleep on the couch. She made herself a sandwich, put away some clothes, and cleaned the bathroom before showering and telling Chris to come to bed. When she walked into the bedroom, she noticed there was a card and a bottle of perfume on the nightstand. The card read, "Happy Birthday."

She looked at the date on her phone and realized that, because of all the hard work on the music, she had missed her own birthday. She felt horrible. She stopped going to the studio for a week; Chris never asked her about it; he just assumed that she had noticed how the pursuit of her dream had affected their relationship.

Regina texted or called every couple of days, asking when Sarah was coming back. It was close to the holidays now, so Sarah said that work was very busy and she didn't have the time or energy to continue working on the last recording.

One day, they were in a cab on the way home and Sarah thought she was hearing things. She asked the driver to turn the radio up, and what do you know? Sarah's song was on the radio. She started crying. She immediately texted Regina and thanked her. Regina replied, "Do I have your attention now?" Sarah replied, "Yes." Chris had a look of disbelief on his face. He was happy, but he wasn't. He knew this was what was supposed to happen, but he wasn't for it. Chris asked Sarah, "Are you happy now?" as if to say, "Now that your song is on the radio, can you give it up now?" Sarah said she was happy, but that she wanted more. Chris wanted more, too, and in that moment, Sarah knew she was in trouble…

There's this saying about how you don't know who really supports you until them supporting you costs them something. Sometimes, success puts a strain on relationships. Sometimes, with success come hate, jealousy, envy, and all the nasty things that can tear even the strongest of bonds apart. Sometimes, this is the reason why some of us aren't as successful as we could be. Sometimes, we put success on the back burner because we know that the hardest thing in the world to do is to manage success and love when only one of you is successful, but both of you are in love.

Dear Woman,

Don't be afraid to get your heart broken.
Be afraid when you stop fighting.
Fighting for what you believe in.
For what you built as your expectations.
Your limitations. Your crown.
That's when you should be nervous:
When you water down your "woman."
When you swallow your pride,
just to wake up to somebody by your side,
or to please a man who finds new ways to disappoint you
three days after you forgive him for the old ones.
So, you put your "womanhood" on ice
when you get lonelier at night.
The winter usually has some of the coldest ones.
When they said, "Keep your enemies close,"
they weren't talking about your bedroom.
If you don't know that, one day, he's going to get on his knees
for you,
how can you possibly give your head to him?
Or your bed to him?
You can't keep lying down with lies,
wondering why you're waking up with disappointments.

"Who's Driving?"

"You are in total control of your life; the second you stop believing that is the second you give someone else the keys."

Every person subconsciously creates barriers. We do it because you can't bring everybody home. Everybody gets lonely, too. This puts people in a tough position. Where most go wrong is assuming that, just because a person makes it through a couple barriers, that means they get second and third chances to not hurt you again. The problem is, instead of putting a couple of barriers between the two of you, you'll start creating barriers between what you thought you wanted and what you have.

Where so many people go wrong is that, when they think about love, they always use a different level of thinking. Everything else is pretty cut-and-dried, but when it comes to love, many of us don't use the same common sense, the same attitude, or the same courage to walk away as we would with anything else.

"If you start treating love like you've been treating everything else in your life, you might just start being as successful in love as you are in everything else in your life."

Have you ever been in the market for a new car? It's a good feeling, right? You sit down in front of a computer, and you start looking at cars online, reading reviews, and asking friends about their cars. Then, when you finally figure out the car you want, you start picturing yourself in it and planning your first trip—you can't wait to show all your friends, and even your enemies. (We're not going to sit here and act like everything we do is done with nothing but good intentions because we both know that's a lie. If you know deep down in your heart that there are some people that you just want to "stunt on," stunt away, just do it tastefully).

While in the market for this new car, you've got the make and model and maybe even the color you want picked out. Now, all you have to do is find it. So, you get out and go to different car lots looking to find your car. Here is where things get tricky. You get to the lot, and you meet the car salesman. You tell the guy or the lady at the lot, "I want a 2011..." and right there, boom!

Barrier. Now he or she can say they don't have that car, and you can say, "Okay, thank you," and walk off the lot, or you can let them continue and say, "However, I do have this 2012 that I think you'll like." Another barrier.

This might be the third or fourth car lot you've visited, it might be late, and you might be tired, so you oblige and say, "Let me see it." Barrier three.

You check out this car, sit in it, and drive it around the block, and then you get back to the dealership. Now, you have another choice: Do I want the car that I'd decided I wanted, or do I want the car that I'm in? Barrier four.

You begin to notice the more of your barriers this car salesman breaks down, the more comfortable he becomes. He will take what you thought was your dream car and give you 300 reasons why you shouldn't buy it, and another 150 why this one is better. He wouldn't have said that to you when you first walked on that lot, now would he? No, because he didn't feel that the two of you were comfortable enough for him to talk you out of your dreams. It wasn't until you didn't walk away after he told you that he didn't have what you were looking for that he was confident enough to try and convince you to agree to something different.

What you've got to understand is, every time you step onto a car lot is just like every time you date a man—you've got to be willing to get your heart broken. Plus, I need you to believe that the sooner this heartbreak happens, the better off you'll be. That car salesman has one job: to sell cars. His job is not to make people's dreams come true; it's not to give people what they ask for, especially when what they ask for is not what he has available. It's your job to know what you want before you even walk onto that lot.

The more of your barriers you let this man break down, the more difficult it's going to be to walk away, because you'll begin to feel comfortable. It's a trap. If you're going to get your heart broken, do it at the dealership—before you sign any papers, before you invest any time, before you spend any money. If not, you might just buy that car because you're tired of walking, tired of looking, tired of waiting. It won't hit you until you're at a red light and you look over in the lane next to you at the car you wanted—the exact color, the exact year. Then, you'll have to ask yourself, "Why didn't I just wait?"

Dear Woman,

A part of falling in love
is knowing when to fall out.
It's knowing when to pull the car over,
and being confident enough to open your mouth.
Ask, "Where are we going?"
If you're not satisfied with the answer,
be just as committed
to unbuckling that seat belt and opening the door,
as you were when you unbuckled your jeans
and opened your legs.
It's about knowing when you're being held down
versus when you're being held up.
Though nobody teaches that.
Everyone uses love as an excuse—
an excuse to ask for forgiveness for their mistakes.
Those same people forget:
Yes, love is about understanding;
however, love is also about them
not putting you in that position
to even have to make the call in the first place.
Give the good years to the good people,
instead of wasting your good tears on the bad ones.

Dear Woman,

There's nothing like a woman who can feed herself.
One who will always appreciate a man's generosity,
but who never needs his help.
A woman soft enough to allow a man to put her on
a pedestal
but strong enough to stand on her own two feet.
Any woman who walks the Earth with her hand out
has to be prepared for whatever people put in it.
Don't let material things blind you
from seeing what his purpose is for you.
Every hand isn't there to help,
and not all gifts come from God.
The problem with charity is,
it's usually people giving up the things they have the most of.
So, you've got an obligation—
a duty to put yourself in a position
where you pay your own way.
A lot of people do things for you
just to be able to remind you that they did them.
They need to know that you can fly on your own.
They need to know that your party is still going to happen,
whether they show up or not.
Letting a man know that you don't need him
makes the real ones excited,
and the weak ones run.

"Holes in Your Armor"

---

*"Men run like water, and like water, they will find
the smallest hole to get through to you."*

Dating is a process all on its own. I have my reservations about some of the principles that are associated with it, but that's a conversation for another time. What I want to talk about now are "ships": friendships, partnerships, relationships, or "situationships;" they all have the same ending in common. I don't know if it was done intentionally or not, but that ending is so perfect for peoples' places in your life.

Let's say that instead of being people, we are all ships. When you think about a ship, water is a ship's best friend, but it can also be its worst enemy. It's just the same way with people. So, you are this ship, floating along, riding these waves of life—you have some days where you might be riding some rough waves and other days where it's just smooth sailing. That's understandable, right? You know they have that saying about how smooth seas never make for a skilled sailor, so it's really about how well you do in those tough times that will determine how well you sail this ship—whatever type it might be.

About that water—as much as the water is your friend, it's also the one thing that can take your ship under. There is no ship on Earth that can't be sunk, some are just stronger than others; some are made up of better materials, some took longer to build, and some have old-fashioned qualities. All of these things are designed so that a ship stands the best chance possible of not getting sunk.

I hope I'm not losing anybody, because here is where things are going to start getting deep (Slight pun intended). The bigger the ship and the more skillful the sailor, the farther away the ship can get from land before it feels uncomfortable. Sort of like us, right?

When we are younger, our parents have our backs; they allow us to experience the world, and we have the opportunity to go back home when things get rough, sort of like day trips. If you were to go out on your boat, the weather might be bad, and the way your ship is built now, you just might not be able to handle it. You're still young and inexperienced, so you take it as a lesson and get yourself back to safety before that water gets in and swallows you whole. As you get older, though, things begin to change; when your ship is too big to fit in the dock, you've got to find a new place to put it. Sometimes it's down the street, sometimes it's on the other side of the world.

Now you're out here on the water, and you don't have the protection from the world that you did when you were just going out on those day trips. If you have some rough sailing weather or if you get into any trouble, you're pretty much on your own. The good thing is, this is how you'll learn how to take care of yourself, because the world is 70 percent water, and you're just one little boat out here trying to find another dock to call home. Along the way, you are going to go through some things with this water. Some days, you're going to wake up, and it's going to be so pretty to look at. Some nights, it's going to rock you to sleep. The trouble comes when you have holes in your ship. What I mean by this is:

"Just like the water tests the integrity of your ship, some of these men out here will test the integrity of your 'woman.' They will find any and every way to get in to sink you. You can't let that happen. Like the water, a real man's job is not to try and sink your ship, but to provide smooth sailing."

You have a responsibility to leave no holes in your armor of womanhood that show weakness. You must be sure to keep a tight ship. Men will take advantage of you. You'll start taking on water and, eventually, they will swallow you whole. If they see you're low on money, they'll use theirs to gain access. They'll see that you've been out here on this water for a long time by yourself; they'll do their best to convince you that these waves are too much for a woman to handle on her own. You might be lost and looking for direction; they'll tell you how they've been there and want to help show you the way. You must give them zero room because all it takes is one hole.

All it takes is one area of weakness, one drop of vulnerability, one opportunity for you to let them onto your boat, and they will turn that hole into a crater. Then, instead of floating above the water, you'll be sinking.

The worst thieves aren't the ones that break into your home and steal your television,

*The worse thieves are the ones you let **break into your heart** and steal your **joy.***

Dear Woman,

What good is being a trophy if you never leave the case?
A princess who never leaves her castle
can never be a ruler.
At best, a Rapunzel.
Don't ever let love leave you all dressed up
with nowhere to go.
When it's real,
you'll never have to worry
about him hiding you from the world.
You'll be his favorite part.
Any man who wins the lottery,
yet doesn't want to spend the money,
he either doesn't appreciate the blessing,
or
he is not capable of handling the attention it brings.
Either way,
this place isn't the place for you.
What good is him giving you the world
if he doesn't have "space" for you?
Some men are hunters,
but no woman should ever be prey.

"Trapped in Paradise"

"Sometimes, heaven is not where you go, but what you make of where you are."

D o you remember the movie *Pretty Woman*? It's a classic, right? If you don't know it, after you're finished reading this book, you should go check it out. Without giving too much of it away, there was this woman going through life, flying by the seat of her pants, just floating in the wind, looking for her next "adventure." Along the way, she meets this very handsome, very rich guy, who ultimately offers to give her the world. I know, I know, every young girl's dream. The movie itself is a little bit more complicated than that, but you'll have to find that out for yourself. What I want to talk about is how that offer can sometimes not be a good thing.

Along this long walk into womanhood, you're going to meet many different types of people. Hopefully, you will be diverse enough in your approach to the men that you select that you'll get a sample of the many different varieties there are. You'll meet foreign guys and local ones; tall, short, brown, black, pink, blue, smart, not so smart, rough, smooth, shy, bold, broke, and RICH.

Let's talk about these rich guys. Now, I'm not picking on them at all. Who doesn't want to be rich? There are many people who are not willing to do some of the things that some people do to become rich, but there isn't a person on this Earth who, if given an opportunity to have enough money to do whatever they pleased for the rest of their life while not having to change one thing about themselves, wouldn't do it. Period.

"Money is like a spare tire: it's not a necessity, but when you need it, you're glad that it's there."

To push the envelope even further, I'm going to ask you to not be intimidated by men who have money. Not all men with money are bad. The fact that a man has money isn't bad; it's what he may want you to do for it, where he wants to take you with it, and what he makes you leave behind that is usually what destroys a weak woman. Be cautious of a man with more money than morals.

Money makes him rich, but it doesn't make him loyal. Nonetheless, just like any other man, he, too, may deserve opportunity.

If you're a good woman, you might be exactly what that man needs. It's so hard to find a good woman when it is no secret that you're financially stable. The other side of that coin, though, is the fact that not all men think this way. The multitude of potential problems usually present themselves in one of two ways: the Investor or the Collector.

You meet this guy, and he seems decent enough for you to be able to engage with him socially. You two go out, and you have a pretty good time; his financial situation allows for you two to enjoy some pretty nice things, eat in some pretty nice restaurants, and experience life in a way that, depending upon how you have lived, you couldn't even dream of previously. First things first: Don't get caught up in all the lights and cameras so much that you get blinded. Make sure you're able to look past all of that stuff and see him for who he really is. Where it gets tricky is his purpose. He might be the type of guy who uses his money and his affinity for women to form a dangerous combination; dangerous, because none of these things make him see you as unique, which means that, eventually, he'll find a new project or "hobby" to experience. Then that limo will pull back up to your studio apartment to drop you off and your fantasy ride will be over. The good news then is that it's over; the bad news is that it shouldn't have happened in the first place. You need to understand for yourself and make him understand that you were doing just fine before he arrived and that you would much rather have a sidekick than a savior.

The other possibility, which is a far more dangerous situation than the first, is that many rich men's wives, girlfriends, and children's mothers live with their men for years, sometimes decades, before they finally break free. This is because the man is a hunter. The hunter is one of the most silent and deadly men out there; silent, because he's not as easy to spot as an outwardly abusive person or an unfaithful person. He's the one who won't do much of anything wrong as it pertains to how he treats you. It will be more about how he *doesn't* treat you after he has you. Let me explain.

So, you meet this Collector. He has all the same qualities as the Investor, but what makes him more dangerous is the fact that he won't ever get bored like the Investor will. He will use all of his "resources" to make you feel as comfortable as he can. It will almost appear to be an infatuation with you; you two will begin hot and heavy and see each other all the time, and if you're not face to face, you'll be phone to phone or fingertip to fingertip. He will make you feel you are the most important thing in his life. He will make it seem like he doesn't know how he managed to function without you, and you will be amazed that someone with so much going for themselves is so caught up in you. It can feel like the perfect combination. What woman doesn't want to feel wanted? That's probably one of every woman's top five feelings that she wants to feel from her partner.

In any event, the infatuation will continue. What started off as dropping you off around 3–4 a.m. will turn into you packing an overnight bag. Weekend getaways will turn into you having your own set of keys, "just in case," along with the top two drawers in his dresser.

DEAR WOMAN,

I feel bad for you.
Every day you wake up,
you are one step closer to dying.
If that's not depressing enough,
every night your pillow is wetter than Miami summers,
melting Popsicles,
and swimming pools.
No matter how much you hate to admit it,
you are in love with a person who's not even trying.
Who doesn't do anything exceptional except lying.
It's killing you.
Faster than aggressive cancer.
Sadder than strong grandmothers with Alzheimer's.
While you put up more of a fight
than addict mothers in rehab
trying to get clean for their babies.
Baby, love doesn't work like that.
Some battles are won by not even going to war.
The loudest thing you can ever give is your silence.
The problem with arguing with a brick wall
is that it cannot hug you after it's over.

DEAR WOMAN,

Sometimes, you've got to ask yourself some tough questions:

"What do I bring to the table?"

"What makes me worthy enough to be with the man
I desire?"

"Would I be happy
if I were the woman your son brought home?"

Some of these women want kings, but they aren't queens.

A clock that doesn't tick is just decoration.

Being a housewife
is knowing how to care for your house and your husband.

Any woman can be the dessert.

Can you bring home the bacon?

Do you know what to do with it?

Before you create a list,
ask yourself what you're looking for in a man.

Ask what a man will see in you.

How complete are you?

Are you waiting for a man to save the day?

A real woman would save herself.

Ask yourself what you bring to the table.

Then, figure out who you're going to eat with.

Dear Woman,

Some of them are going to hate you regardless.
So, let your grind speak for itself.
Social media be your toilet.
Show no mercy.
The rules say be humbled, not dead.
You don't have to let them know
who and what you're doing—
just that you're not lonely but well-fed.
Let them keep their eyes on you.
You just keep your eyes on your own paper
until you can wake up one day
and have to get in your car
to see your next-door neighbors.
A lot of these women just have
too much time on their hands.
Not you—
you've got your grind on your hands.
Be so busy clocking your accomplishments
that you don't have time for a man.
A woman who can feed herself will have men
eating from the palm of her hand.

"Fuel"

"What people say about you says a lot more about them than it does about you."

It is perfectly all right to broadcast your blessings. Under no circumstances should you ever in a million years downplay your greatness because you don't want to hurt anybody's feelings. It's a tough job, but somebody has to do it. Just make sure you do it with style and class. Don't be sorry for what you do have, be sorry that they are more worried about what you have than about what they don't. You can't spend your life walking on other peoples' eggshells, especially when everything you've gotten thus far has been from hard work, dedication, and good genes.

If you have a good job, a nice apartment, a great sense of fashion, and a dope smile, you need to share that with the world. You know why? For every hater, there is another woman you can inspire. For everyone who has something negative to say about you or what you do, there is someone willing to go to bat for you. If people have taken the time out of their day to speak about you, then you must be doing something right. Right? So, keep doing what you're doing. They are going to watch anyway, so you might as well give them a show.

When dealing with hate, the only time you lose is when you lose your composure. When you get off your throne to address a peasant, you give them satisfaction. Satisfaction is something you should reserve for the people who are inspired by you. If you don't have any of those people around you, find some. You have to learn how not to keep your ear so close to the ground that you won't be able to hear God tell you how proud of you He is. Let them talk. As long as they keep guessing, they'll never know.

If you had a choice between spending a day signing autographs and a day answering hate mail, which would you do? Some of these bullies only bother you because you allow yourself to be bothered. Let your actions and your transactions speak for themselves. Nine times out of ten, the person who's keeping score usually isn't winning. So, you keep rising above it and racking up the air miles.

DEAR WOMAN,

The worst ones are the ones who get used to it.

If you eat too much of anything, you'll begin to love it.

*A woman dies every time she replaces "forget you" with
"forget it."*

You keep a bird in a cage too long,

eventually, it will forget how to fly.

You keep hurting a woman in the same way,

eventually, she'll forget how to cry.

"He keeps calling," she said.

Even bad men love, too.

It's not a question of whether or not he loves you,

*it's about how much disappointment comes with his
"I love you."*

*You think the devil is just going to let you walk out of hell
without a fight?*

He's going to do whatever it takes to keep you.

*It's your job as a woman not to confuse DESERVE
with DESIRE.*

Some bridges are meant to be burned.

They're just waiting on you to light the fire.

"The Drag"

"Life isn't over when you die; it's over when you stop trying to live."

There is a distinct difference between a man who wants you and a man who doesn't want to see you with anybody else. Never forget that. How do you know? It's simple. As a woman, your presence should be appreciated at all times. It shouldn't take your leaving or even your threatening to leave, for a man to give you reasons to stay. The most dangerous word in the dictionary is "love," especially when what you love or who you love doesn't love like you love. This is when your love gets used against you. You have to pay attention, because the really good ones—not good as in *good*, but good as in bad—they don't just run up on you and rip your crown off your head. That's too obvious, and any woman can see that coming a mile away.

What do they do? They chip away at your crown until there is nothing left. Then, you'll feel like it's you and not them. It's so deep of a thing that I'm surprised some men are so good at it. Then again, they put a monkey on the moon, so at this point anything is possible. I'm going to do you a favor and let you know how it goes down:

It starts off with an infatuation that piques your interest. I mean, what woman doesn't like to be desired? In reality, though, that's his way in. It's so much easier to rob anybody of anything when you're on the inside.

Once he's in, the changes will be subtle. It will be more of a *test the water* type of thing—like when babies test their parents to see how far they can go before they get in trouble. It's done to see how much control he has. Step two is getting in and taking control. That's when you begin to be chipped away. You know that saying about how some men only want you until they've got you? It's sort of the opposite when it comes to some men. We are the first to fall in, and you, women, are always the last to fall out.

He'll notice where he can get over on you, and that's where the chipping begins. It's sort of like when we talked about the "holes in your armor." What messes up most women is that there is a give-and-take component that comes with the chipping. He will give you BS and then take you shopping. It might not be shopping—

it could be whatever he knows your weakness is. Eventually, the taking will become more and the giving will become less. Unfortunately, the same things that make some women better than some men can ultimately be your downfall. It will be your level of understanding and compassion, mixed with the fact that this isn't your first rodeo with a man who falls short of your expectations. You'll just chalk it up as "men being men" and pray that one day he gets it. What you need to understand is that you must make sure he "gets it" before he "gets" *you*. Otherwise, you'll be in what's known as "the drag." That's when everything goes downhill.

The drag is the point in a relationship where a man does exactly that to a woman: he drags her. More specifically, it's when he knows he's got you, and he doesn't even have to keep doing what he did to get you to keep you. Does that make sense? Basically, the only thing keeping you there is your loyalty, your love, and your stupidity. I tried to think of a nicer word, but I couldn't. The drag is the point of the relationship where you're literally hanging on while he's taking you wherever he wants to go, and those three words are like the rope that ties you to the bumper of the car. Every so often, he might pull the car over and cut you some slack, but that's because he doesn't want to pop the rope. He'll pull over long enough to take you some place nice and have one of those pep talks with you about how he's trying and how he needs you to be more understanding. You'll feel motivated, but it's false hope. This will happen roughly three to four times a month. More than likely, it will end with him having sex with you. Then while you were asleep, he's gone and got himself some fresh rope and tied you up, and by the time you wake up and come to your senses, you're back on the drag line again.

The crazy part is, the whole time, you had a box cutter in your back pocket. Who knew? That box cutter is your pimp juice; it's your swagger. You discover it in that moment when he goes just a little too far. It will be the equivalent of him rolling over some rocks while dragging you and you bumping your head. Sometimes you've got to be dragged through it to get through. The good news is, now you've come to your senses. Then what do you do?

To be honest, some women won't cut the rope and run the other way. That would be too easy. The insecure ones will cut the rope off and just sit in the middle of the road, waiting for him to realize he's traveling a little bit lighter. Sadly, then they'll wait for him to catch on and come back. Sometimes it's because such a woman thinks that, now that he knows she can escape the drag line, he might not drag her anymore, or it could be that wherever he was dragging her to is way better than where she came from, so she's got to wait for him to come back. She just hopes that maybe she can go in the trunk instead. Either way, she's screwed.

The other type of woman is the one who pulls out the box cutter, cleans herself up, and stands on the side of the road; then she shows a little leg and picks up some guy, telling him to follow the car that was dragging her. Not only that, when the car pulls over, she hops back out and ties herself to the rope again. She doesn't want him to know she knows how to get away or that a new little "AAA" friend came to her rescue. Trust me, it happens. Why? Maybe she thinks that one day he's going to get tired of dragging her. In the beginning, he was a good guy, so she may just want to stick around, thinking that one day he might come to his senses. It never happens.

Your best bet is not to let yourself get dragged. Second best, keep that box cutter in your pocket early on, because you're too pretty to be rolling through the mud. Number three, always keep AAA!

DEAR WOMAN,

To think that your heart
will never get broken is foolish.
I mean, honestly,
how many things have you ever gotten right
on the first try?
I bet you don't even remember.
I bet you do remember that one thing
you never quit doing until you got it right.
Right? Exactly.
Look, the truth is, nobody knows a damn thing about love
until we're knee-deep in it with the wrong person.
So, the question isn't, "Will you get your heart broken?"
The question is, "What are you going to do after?"
The only two things you have on this Earth
are your heart and hope.
To give them away is foolish.
To lose them is a sin.
They say, learn from your mistakes,
not live with them.

"Rainbows"

_____

"One more time."

_____

I knew she was in trouble when the first thing she said to me was, "I don't want to fall in love ever again." It wasn't so much the look on her face or the tone of her voice that made me nervous. It was when I looked into her eyes and saw that beneath her lashes, there were tears. There were enough tears that, as soon as I gave her my shoulder, I placed a bucket beneath our feet to catch the pain. She never cried when she was with him. So, when she finally let it out, it was for every text message to his phone from a "friend" at 2 a.m. that disrupted both her sleep and her sense of security. It was for every girl who walked past her in the mall and stared just a little too hard, whose body language whispered, "I know something that you don't." The saddest part was not that he let her down, but that she held him up so high in the first place. She never asked him to be perfect, just loyal. Loyalty, to a boy who doesn't know its definition or her worth, is like asking for Chick-Fil-A on a Sunday. No matter how strong the desire may be, some things are just beyond your control.

To make matters worse, after she dried her eyes, she posed a question to me. She asked, "Am I wrong if I still love him?" I replied that love is a feeling that transcends even the people for whom you have it. It's the understanding of the definition and applying it to a person in hopes that the two of you share its responsibilities and its expectations. After that, it becomes an agreement to execute its duties equally. In other words, love is an action word. If there are no actions that can prove the word, then the word itself is just a word.

I asked her why she still loved him. She replied that they had been together for years. I told her that, when the slaves were finally freed, many of them never left the plantation, not because they didn't know they were free, but because freedom comes with a responsibility to walk away from everything you knew—the second you knew it didn't deserve you. She told me that by the way I was speaking, I couldn't have ever been in love before. I said to her, "Love is a road you travel down from the day you are born until the day you die. Every person you meet is an intersection. Some just cross your path; others go along for the ride. If every time someone decided that they no longer wanted to walk this path with you, you decided to follow them instead of getting to your destination, then you would forever be lost."

Then, she asked, "How many times can you get knocked down before you stay down?" From the pain in her voice, you could tell that this wasn't the first man she had given her heart to who didn't know what to do with it. I told her that all she had to do was stand up one more time—heal one more time. Try loving again once more. That's all it takes: one more time. You've got to be willing to invest in love, the same amount you did the first time, every time. Love is a gamble, but all it takes is for you to place your bet one more time, and you'll be rich forever.

DEAR WOMAN,

Sometimes, you bite off more than you can chew.

Your eyes become bigger than your stomach.

You knew he was out of your league from the beginning.

You decided to lace up your sneakers and play anyway.

Now you're mad that you lost at a game you didn't have any

business playing in the first place.

You were just tired of sitting on benches.

When you don't stretch before you play,

you might not feel it during the game,

but the next morning, you might not be able

to make it out of bed.

Before you know it,

you can't even manage to get him out of your head.

It's funny, because if you had used your head in

the beginning,

you wouldn't have even been in this situation.

You dove head first into a pool you couldn't see the bottom of.

After you got hurt, you blamed him

for not being deep enough for you.

Yet you couldn't even be responsible enough

to check the writing on the wall or the side of the pool.

The funny thing about leading with your heart

is that if it doesn't work,

it's going to be the first thing that gets hurt.

Just because the ball is in your court,

doesn't mean you have to shoot.

You can't love a player but hate the game.

You can't expect to beat a professional if you're so new

you're still just a number without a name.

Now, you're trying to convince yourself it was his fault.
When you stick your hand in a lion's cage,
you lose all control of what happens after.
The scariest part about love is leaving your heart
in someone else's hands.
Understanding that to do it the right way,
you must give up all control.
So, if you wouldn't give your child to any sitter,
your car to any mechanic,
or the keys to your apartment to someone
you're not sure will leave it just the way they found it,
treat love like it's your last dollar.
If they don't value your investment enough
to turn it into $2,
make sure they respect you enough
to give your $1 back to you.

You two are either going to get married or break up.
The only question is when?
Summer is going to turn into winter.
One year is going to turn into four.
The top drawer in each other's dresser
Is going to turn into a twelve-month lease,
The cable in your name,
The electric in his,
And a two-year-old baby girl.
Then,
One day you'll wake up, roll over,
Look him dead in the eye
And realize that, this whole time,
You were settling.

Dear Woman,

There comes a point in every man's life when he finally
"gets it."
Some take months, some take years. All feel like forever.
You just have to ask yourself if he's worth taking the
ride with.
Sometimes, it's the one that has made you cry already
that cares the most about sparing your tears.
There comes a point in every man's life when he understands
that it's not about being "the man;" it's about being "a man."
It's up to you to believe him.
It's up to you to decide what it is you need to fix you.
Do you need love or do you need him?
After you've figured that out,
and he's still an option,
the only question is, are you willing to give him
the opportunity?
If there's still love there, I say go for it.
Love is like college,
what good is going through all these tests,
if you can't one day walk across the stage
and have something to show for it?
If you keep switching majors, a lot of the credits you've
earned aren't going to transfer.
If the pain is too much for you to deal with, that's okay.
While he may not deserve an opportunity,
the least you can do is give him an answer.

Dear Woman,

I need you to promise me something.
Promise me that you will never leave your heart
in the palms of a man
who has not made his purpose for you clearer
than your grandmother's bathroom window.
Promise me that who you love
will never be more important
than the love you have for yourself.
You cannot give shelter to others
if you do not have a home of your own.
Promise me that you won't settle.
No matter how little your job pays,
no matter how small your apartment is.
You are one good man away
from being treated like a queen.
No matter where on Earth your castle is,
and despite every man who ever broke your heart—
may their Karma and your peace
be God allowing them the pleasure
of receiving front-row tickets to your rebirth.

"Restaurant Week"

"Variety is the spice of life!"

W hat's your favorite food? Not to cook, but if you were to go to a restaurant, what is your meal of choice? Mine would be Fettuccini Alfredo, with extra Alfredo sauce and salmon and shrimp (thank me later). Anyway, in Philadelphia, twice a year, they have this thing called, "Restaurant Week." It's when some of the more exclusive and more expensive restaurants in the city open their doors and slash their prices so that people who otherwise couldn't afford them or didn't know they existed have an opportunity to try something different. Last summer, I participated—sort of. I did go to places I had never heard of to eat. But guess what I ended up ordering? Yup, salmon and shrimp Alfredo. No matter what restaurant I went to, that's what I ordered. I didn't need to see the menu. I didn't care what their specialty was. I didn't want to know what the soup or the fish of the day was or what the person I was with had the last time they were here. I had a tunnel vision appetite. It didn't bother me, though. It was what I wanted. It was my money I was spending, so it was what I got.

Why that? It was the first thing that I'd had that I really liked, so I stuck with it. I actually stuck with it for a long time. I became oblivious to everything else.

I wouldn't go to a restaurant if I knew they didn't serve it. It wasn't until I went to an Italian restaurant that didn't serve Alfredo that my life changed, and I realized how foolish of a mistake I was making. Being forced to step outside of that comfort zone changed my appetite and my life. I fell in love with Chicken Parmesan.

So, today, I'm going to challenge you to step outside of your comfort zone. Sometimes in love, people operate the same way as they do with their food. Assuming you're single, think about the last three men you dated. Ask yourself a question and be honest with yourself:

Did you really date three different men, or did you go to three different restaurants and order the same food?

Finding out what you like in a man is a process. It usually has to do with the first man that you really fall for. Nine times out of ten, it didn't work with him because it is so difficult to meet someone so early on and have it end with you two growing old together. After the breakup, most people usually put the blame on the guy, which in this case would be the restaurant, instead of on the food, which would be what you're looking for in a guy. It really puts you in a tough position.

You had this one guy who kind of set the table for what you thought you wanted in a man. So, you travel the world trying to find that taste again, hoping that you can get the same Alfredo, just from a different place. As I did, you become ignorant to all the other possibilities of the various types of food that you can experience. This is the biggest mistake you can ever make. Why? Exposure to different things can put you in different places. All you have to do is be willing to try something different. The reason I use food as an example is because it really doesn't cost you anything. There is no long-term commitment with dating a different guy, just as there isn't any with trying a different dish. You don't like it, you don't have to finish it. You don't have to take it back home with you, and you don't ever have to go back there again. You almost can't lose. Some things you just know to avoid, both with food and men. So, if you're allergic to shellfish, don't eat seafood. If you're not a fan of flashy, or if overly sensitive guys really aren't your thing, that's totally fine. Just don't limit yourself.

The reason why you might not be able to find true love is because you keep looking for the same version of an old love. There are so many different types of men out there. Good men. Great men. You just have to be willing to say, "You know what, surprise me!" You never know, this could be the best meal you've ever tasted, but you'll never know if you never try it.

*Every woman loves **something** just a little bit more than she should.*

*For some women, it's **chocolate**. For some women, it's some **man**.*

When in doubt, go with the chocolate.

DEAR WOMAN,

Don't spoil your dinner.

Remember when your mother wouldn't let you

eat junk food while she was making dinner?

But you were just so hungry, so impatient,

you just wanted something to eat right away.

Love is the same way.

Just like good food, good love takes time.

Where a lot of people mess up is not being willing to wait.

No good food comes prepared.

No person comes into your life perfectly fit for you.

Once you've figured out what you have a taste for,

gotten all your ingredients, and started cooking,

be patient and let your food cook.

In other words, let your love grow

to a point where it can feed you.

Now you can spoil it

with that bag of Doritos if you want to.

But remember why

you started cooking dinner in the first place.

No one could ever survive on just junk food.

"New Generation, New Woman"

"When the times change, so must the people."

Sometimes, women get caught up in the fairytales, even though those stories were written a long time ago. It's a new day as far as relationships are concerned. With a new day, women have to adopt new understandings about how the process of love works.

The days of a man knocking on the door of your parents' house and telling you how he had a place of his own and he couldn't think of anyone else that he wanted to come home to find barefoot and pregnant besides you are over. You can blame the feminist movement for saying there shouldn't be gender roles, so now men can be stay-at-home dads and women can work fifty to sixty hours a week, or you can blame it on the economy and inflation and say that a family can't survive with only one income anymore. These days, both spouses need to be working every day in order to maintain at least some sort of decent living situation. If you don't have a clue what I'm talking about right now, that's okay. Well, not really—if you don't have a clue, you should really Google feminism, gender roles, and inflation at some point in the next thirty days. Things can be put even more simply by saying that most men these days don't have homes of their own, compounded by the fact that most women now are more lost in the kitchen than they are when watching sports.

No matter how you slice it, stuff has changed, most of it not in a good way, either. I don't want to rain on your parade, but I would be lying if I told you that you should just keep being patient; that the right man is going to come into your life on a white horse, keys to some big mansion in tow, and he's going to pay off all your student loans, fix your credit, and give you an endless supply of MAC cosmetics along with bundles of hair and will always want to take selfies so you can post pictures every Monday and Wednesday. That doesn't even sound possible. The longer you wait for Prince Charming, the more likely you'll be looking like Queen Elizabeth II by the time he gets here.

It's safe to say that you're going to have to be your own superheroine. You're going to have to get your own place, cook your own food, fix your own bathroom sink, and still be able to get cute in the mirror. It's hard to have these old-school expectations with this new generation of guys. Life used to start for a woman when she moved in with her husband. You can wait on that if you want to. I recommend that you get that party started by yourself. Then, if you meet a guy and he's halfway decent, you just invite him over and tell him to bring the ice.

"You don't need a man to come and save the day.
Just one who wants to be your favorite part of it."

That's your best bet. If not, you'll be twirling your thumbs waiting for Superman to come rescue you, but he's bringing ice to Wonder Woman's house.

DEAR WOMAN,

What if I told you that, every morning,
you wake up a virgin all over again?
Would you still be so anxious to get undressed
forty-five minutes after the sun sets
with a man who knows
what your body looks like without clothes,
but has no desire to see you "naked"?
If all the conversations are about coming and going,
you'll never arrive.
If the only thing that's getting fed is your body,
you'll never survive.
If you get on your knees more than he does,
you'll never be a bride.
If the only time he gives you life
is when he gives you pipe,
no matter how deep he plunges,
this situation is still full of waste.
Friends last longer than lovers
because sex without love is just exercise.
It's time for you to exercise your right
to be done with all the foolishness.
You're worth the wait, no matter how long you take.
Find the one who wants to mix ingredients
instead of just being greedy
and wanting a slice of your cake.
Friends last longer than lovers.
Friends turn into family,
lovers turn into babies' mothers.

"Not Good Enough? Impossible!"

"The only woman who will never get what she deserves is the one who doesn't believe she deserves it."

I once met a young woman when I used to live in San Diego whose name was Valerie. Valerie was a 5'2" 110-pound Mexican woman whose parents had moved to a small suburb just south of San Diego called Otay Mesa while her mother was still pregnant with her. Valerie's parents were from Tijuana, which is a city in Mexico just across the border. They wanted the best for Valerie, so they sold everything they owned and moved to America. As it is for many "illegal immigrants," it was difficult for Valerie's parents to find work. No green card meant no real job. So, as many people do who come to our country—"the land of opportunity"—who don't go through the organized channels, Valerie's parents were driven into the construction and service industries. Valerie's father had friends and family in San Diego who were in the same situation. Needing to find work, they would all wake up at 5 a.m. and camp out in front of places like Home Depot and Lowe's in hopes that there would be contractors and customers who needed an extra hand with whatever improvements they were doing. Valerie's mother had two sisters who had been in the area for years, so after she had Valerie, she began working with them cleaning large homes in the La Jolla section of San Diego.

Fast-forward twenty years to when I attended an event at a home in La Jolla. A local fashion designer was launching a new swimsuit line, and they were having a pool party/fashion show at his home. Needless to say, once I heard about it, I was one of the first people there. Don't judge me, I was a different person back then.

I showed up at the party and was in heaven: models in swimsuits to look at, pigs in a blanket to eat, and an open bar. Plus I was off the next day. I was calling everybody I knew and telling them I had hit the jackpot. I went into the bathroom with my third drink in hand. Keep in mind, I had only been there about twenty minutes. (Disclaimer: Alcohol addiction is a dangerous disease. If you need help, please get it). I went into the bathroom because I didn't want anyone to know I was calling my friends.

In a rush to get back to the action, before I could even hang up my phone and take my next breath, I opened the door and there she was—Valerie, standing by the bathroom door, dressed in all black,

wearing a lanyard around her neck that read, "Staff." First thing I
thought was, "Damn, I'm busted." I played dumb and proceeded
to exit the bathroom, headed back to the party. After I had taken
two steps out the door, I realized I'd left my drink behind. So, I
sidestepped her and went to pick it up from the bathroom sink.
Valerie immediately cut me off and said, "It's fine. I have it." I said,
"It's mine, though, but if you want one, I can get it." She declined
and mentioned that they didn't let staff drink. I said, "But every
model in here is drunk." She replied, "Who said I was a model?"
Then she proceeded to pick up a bucket full of cleaning supplies,
enter the bathroom, and clean the toilet.

I said, "If it's dirty, then it wasn't me. I just went in to…" She cut me
off, saying, "You went in to tell your friends there were pretty girls
and free drinks everywhere; you need practice in whispering." I
smiled and walked away.

I really didn't think anything else of it. I was there to have a good
time, and that's exactly what I did. Eventually, my friends came, and
once they got there and saw what was going on, I never received
so many hugs from grown men in my life. We all had girlfriends
then, so we were looking for places to have a good time that
didn't involve a Lifetime movie or a group date. Some of my good
friends were more hands-on than others. I just sat in the back and
watched. I had one of those cool girlfriends who said I could look
all I wanted, just not touch. I had a good woman, so I listened.

While I was sitting and watching the show, I noticed Valerie
was, too. I went over and stood next to her. She didn't pay me
much mind, though; her eyes were glued to the runway. She was
critiquing every model that walked by. Fix your hand, close your
mouth, stop smiling, arch your back… etc. I laughed and said,
"You need to put the mop bucket down and pick up a clipboard.
You should be backstage, not back here."

Her response was, "I don't want to be backstage; I want to be on
stage." The way she said it gave me a chill. Her English might have
been broken, but her spirit was far from it. It's like she believed in
it, the same way all the great ones believe they were great. That's

the first step. Everything else that happens after is hard work and dedication.

I asked what was stopping her, and she replied, "Life." She began to tell me about how a while back, her father had been helping a contractor put on a roof in Carlsbad, and since that wasn't his profession, just what he was doing that day to make ends meet, he didn't have the necessary equipment. So, when he got down to the edge of the roof by the gutter, he stood up to grab another handful of nails, slipped, and fell. The only thing that had saved his life were the bushes he had put in the week prior. Even so, he had ended up being paralyzed from the waist down. That had been three years ago.

She went on to tell me about how her mother and sisters had gotten into an argument about some jewelry that had gone missing from a home they had been cleaning eight months before. The sisters had ended up splitting up their cleaning service. Valerie still worked most days, though, but the reason they were so successful had been that the three of them could clean a five-bedroom house in half a day. Now, it took her mother two days by herself. So, Valerie had been forced to leave school and clean with her mother.

I felt her pain. Sometimes life does get in the way of life. As badly as I wanted to tell her that it was all right to be cleaning up behind rich people all day, and as much as I wanted to make her feel good about sacrificing her dream for the sake of her family, I couldn't.

I told her that she had given me a bunch of reasons why other people's lives weren't being lived to their full potential—not hers. Then I asked her again, "Why don't you model?" That's when she revealed her real truth. She said, "You know why I'm not a model? Fine, I'll tell you. I'm 5'2. I'm Mexican. I don't have a car. I don't have money for photo shoots. I'm always either cleaning at work or cleaning at home. My English is bad, my teeth are crooked, and I don't have any experience. I've been to every agency in this city, and they all say the same thing, I'm just not good enough."

I told her, "After all that, deep down in your heart, you still want
to do it. So, you owe it to yourself, you owe it to your family. Your
parents didn't come here so you could clean toilets. They didn't
come here so you could watch other people pursue their dreams.
Ninety percent of the people out here are dream killers. Ninety
percent of the people out here don't wake up every day to do what
they love. They do what pays the rent, and they do what keeps
the lights on, but in the process, the light inside of them gets
dimmer and darker. Most people will talk you out of your dream
because somebody talked them out of theirs. Negative energy is
contagious, too. Sometimes, things not going our way is a test,
a test to see how bad we really want it. The things that usually
come easily are the things we don't value enough. So, if you don't
believe you're good enough to be a model, stop thinking about
modeling. Stop criticizing other models. If all your life is going
to be about cleaning up after other peoples' messes, then that's
all you need to be worrying about. I'm telling you right now, that
would be a waste of everything you have been blessed with."

Dear Woman,

If you think you're lonely now,
wait until tonight –
when the mixtures of your hormones
and two glasses of wine
has you in heat and in your feelings.
You can't remember the last time
you felt a man's hands
play the piano with your spine,
so you decide to go scrolling
through your contacts,
hoping to catch a contact high
from the rubbing of a man's leg
between your thighs,
only to watch him pull his pants up
before you can even open your lips
and ask him to stay.
It's at that moment that you realize,
the loneliest a woman will ever be
is five minutes after sex,
when the only thing that happens
faster than him coming over
or him coming inside of you,
is him coming to the conclusion
that you're good enough to lay down with,
but not good enough to wake up to.

"Boyfriend by Committee"

"There are a few occasions when a woman can have too many options—one is when all her options have a desire to be the priority."

Some days, she wanted to be spoiled. Other days, she wanted to be motivated to be a better woman by a man who not only saw her potential but understood that the most valuable thing you can do for a woman is not to feed her, but to teach her how to feed herself. Some days, she wanted her mind explored; some nights, just her body. She wanted it all, and rightfully so. Yet, wanting it all was not the problem. The problem was that it didn't matter who she got it from.

In some ways, love and happiness are like empty cups. We all have them in our hands, and we are waiting for somebody to fill them up with what matches our expectations of what we desire in a partner. The longer the cups stay empty, the more impatient a woman becomes. When the thirst becomes too great, instead of waiting, she'll find a man who may have merely a sample of what she is ultimately looking for. The sample will only be just enough to quench her thirst for the moment, enough to fulfill only one of her desires. The trouble comes when, instead of waiting for a glass that is overflowing with possibility, she starts taking shots: shots of motivation, shots of stimulation, shots of attention, shots of affection. These shots will be filled to the brim with that one flavor of love that you're looking for. While it might taste good, remember that it is still just a shot. Since you're thirsty, the bartenders, all seven or eight of them, keep filling up your cup. The good news is, you're no longer thirsty. The bad news is, the bill is going to come. Then whom do you pay?

I want you to know I know how hard it is to find someone who is going to be that one cup that's overflowing. It's going to seem like it's taking forever. The longer it takes, the more you'll want it. Of course, the process of finding that one cup involves dating. While you're dating, you're going to come across some people who you know may not be capable of being that glass every woman so desperately craves, but who would serve as a pretty decent shot of one thing that you may want in that glass. I need you to be strong enough not to take it, for a couple of reasons:

1. Sometimes, when you get a shot of something that you know is one of the things you want in your glass, you become foolishly satisfied. It's foolish because you're smart enough to know that this is only a shot, so you're still out there looking for your glass. However, since the taste is still in your mouth, you tend to stop looking for it, while you're out there looking for the glass. So foolishly, you'll continue to date, and that won't be one of the things you're looking for because you'll think you already have it. Guess what? You don't.

2. When you show a guy it's all right for him to be just a shot, when he knows you're out here looking for a cup, but you drink that shot anyway, you're in even more trouble. Why? Nine times out of ten, when he is a shot, he's probably a shot of something of which he has an abundance, so as soon as you drink it, by the time you put that shot glass on the table, he's already poured you another one. You might get so drunk that you can't even see straight—too much of something is never good because it takes room away from something else. Then you're getting a shot of this from over here and a shot of that from over there, until you get so full off of shots that you might not even be thirsty anymore.

3. Last, but most certainly not least, the bill is going to come. All of the men you've gotten all these shots from—none of which were forced down your throat, by the way—are all going to want something in return. Then what will you do? Whose desires will you fulfill? Before you know it, you'll have five or six shot glasses on the table, all of them wanting you, and you just wanting a cab ride home.

DEAR WOMAN,

Love is like a casino.
The quarters: Your heart.
The people you date: The machines.
Just like money, most of us don't have
endless amounts of love to give.
So, if you've been at this same machine,
feeding it quarter, after quarter, after quarter,
and you still have not "won,"
maybe it's time to try a new machine.
Once you're out of quarters, you're broke(n).
No one should go broke trying to get rich.

"Mommy's Baby"

"You'll never know how strong you are, until strong is the only option you have."

She wishes.
She wishes she had the same baby.
Just with a different daddy.
It's hard for her to explain to her child that
"Daddy didn't start acting 'funny'
till after Mommy had you."
She wishes.
She wishes she could have played pretend with Daddy.
Had she known that Daddy was going to disappear
before they actually had the baby,
she would have only "pretended"
to not use a condom.
Instead of pretending now
that her baby doesn't need a daddy.

L ord knows that no woman has ever decided to lie down with a man and, just before she unsnapped her bra and removed her underwear, said to herself, "If I get pregnant and I have to end up raising a child all by myself, I will not complain." That just doesn't happen. What does happen is a woman underestimates a man's ability to be nothing like what he advertises himself to be.

She doesn't take into consideration while she's making love to him that the same number of men who talk the talk will never be the same number who end up walking it. Sad, but most certainly true.

There is a lot of fingerpointing that could have been done toward everyone involved—from the time she met the man to the time that she met the product of meeting the man. All of that is irrelevant now, because you can't cry over spilled milk, and a child alone has enough tears and requires enough milk to go around.

So now we're here at a point in a woman's life that she could never be prepared for, no matter how many times she's witnessed it on television or in her neighborhood, or even if she is a product of it herself. Single parenthood is a crash course that will most certainly be learned as you go through it. The most important requirement is that you do indeed go. There are lot of theories and criticism that put a false sense of fear into women's, especially young women's, heads and hearts about raising kids alone. I don't have to list them because I'm sure you've heard them all. You've probably heard some I haven't. Obviously, every woman who reads this book isn't for sure a mother, but I assume that most plan, one day, to become one. So, what I'm going to do is break this down in a way that applies to all of you in some way.

Here goes…

Operation Scared Straight: I'm pretty sure most of you are familiar with the term, the youth program, or the television show "Scared Straight." If not, it's basically a concept that was created by juvenile courts as a method of deterring at-risk youth who have been arrested for minor crimes by requiring them to visit a local prison and meet with people serving long sentences as a means to deter them from committing more crimes. The visit includes seeing what the inside of a cell looks like, being forced to wear the uniform, meeting the inmates, etc. Of course, many of these interactions between the children and the inmates as well as the prison staff are exaggerated, but it's all done with an agenda of "scaring them straight." The problem is, children have become smarter and bolder, and nowadays they see this program as more of a joke.

You know what isn't a joke? Dropping out of high school during senior year because, as badly as you want to get up and go to class, you just can't. Your daughter kept you up until 4 a.m. because she wouldn't stop crying. She was crying because the first bottle you made was too hot. Then you made another one. But by the time you gave it to her, it was too cold. It was too cold because when you walked back into the bedroom, you realized she had thrown up all over herself. She threw up on herself because you'd put her down too fast after she had eaten. You put her down too fast because you forgot the bottle was on the stove. Then you had to change her onesie. While you were putting the new one on her, this smell hit you like a ton of bricks. The smell was the other half of that baby food that you gave her earlier that she didn't throw up. So, then, you had to change her diaper. Speaking of diapers, did you know that a newborn goes through fifteen diapers a day? That's 450 a month. That costs about $210—not including wipes, baby powder, clothes, shoes, copays for doctors' visits, milk, food, strollers, toys, medicine, soap, and lotion. You see where I'm going with all this? Good.

So, when you hear people preach to you about not rushing into it, you see where they are coming from, right? A lot of the shows and documentaries about how hard it is being a single mom understand they're doing a job. They're trying to save you. You know that mom who keeps talking to you about safe sex, birth control, and condoms? She's trying to save you. Don't let some parts of your life be over too soon because others have started too soon. Nobody's saying a woman can't raise a child on her own; all we're saying is, why would you want to?

Operation Anyway. If you missed the boat on all the motivational scare tactic stuff about how raising a child on your own is almost impossible, and how a woman can't raise a boy to be a man, you heard it, but didn't listen; or you listened, but didn't think it could ever happen to you, until it did happen to you, and now you're looking into the eyes of the most beautiful thing you've ever seen in your entire life. Yet, you don't know the first thing about being a single parent. All you know is that you're in love. I want you to know that anything anyone ever told you, anything you ever heard about how you're not going to be able to do it, is a lie. It's a lie because they don't know how much you love your baby. They don't know how having this baby changed your life. They don't know how in giving birth, in some ways, you gave birth to yourself, too; a new you, a you that is going to beat the odds, a you that is going to make it anyway. There isn't a child out here who couldn't use an active father, but there isn't a mother out here who will ever let her child feel like they are missing something. This party must and will go on. Regardless of who is supposed to come, who is running late, and who never shows up, you can't worry about what you don't have just because you don't have it.

You have an obligation to be the best damn mother you can be, in spite of circumstances. Obligation supersedes any negativity. Just when you think it's too much to handle, just when you think you're alone, creep into their bedroom, sit on the floor, and watch them sleep. Look at how peaceful they look. You did that. Let that peace give you peace.

If you need any evidence of how a woman can raise a boy to be a man, look to me. I am proof; proof that it's possible—proof that the only boy a woman can't raise to be a man is the boy who thinks he's a man already. Raise royalty, and if you have to do it alone, fear not, because at least you get to take all the credit. I love you and I'm praying for you.

DEAR WOMAN,

To all the women who do it alone, I respect you.

Never let your baby's father or his failures affect you.

To all the women who CHOOSE to do it alone,

only because it never worked out the way you wanted it to,

trying to turn "playing house" into a home,

so, now, you won't even let him talk

to his children on the phone:

Shame on you.

There are over four million women under forty

with a "baby daddy" who is either dead or in prison.

Another sixteen million more who just don't care.

So, for you to use his son as a bargaining chip,

or to deprive your daughter of the first man

she's supposed to fall in love with just ain't fair.

You like calling yourself a single mom,

like it's an accomplishment.

Only thing you're accomplishing

is making your child's life more difficult.

You can't force something that's just not there.

You're dead wrong if you have a man

who wants to be a father to his kids,

yet the kid in you can't be mature about the situation.

You situate yourself in child support court,

letting someone who wasn't in the bedroom

when you were making that child

tell you how much your son is worth

and the schedule of visitation.

When parents play tug of war,

the child always loses.

When he stopped, she stopped.
He stopped giving her flowers.
He stopped calling just to hear her voice.
He stopped telling her she looked beautiful.
He stopped doing what it took
to get her after he got her.
That will be how he loses her.
Don't get the girl that everybody wants,
then forget that she's still
the girl that everybody wants.

DEAR WOMAN,

The scariest part about love
is the fact that, more than likely,
you will always fall into it together.
Quickly and without a care.
The whole world will be your audience.
The two of you will be the stars of the show.
Every morning will feel like
your favorite Saturday cartoon,
and every night, your favorite love movie.
Every Friday will feel like prom all over again:
When the only feeling better than your best friend
helping you put on your dress
was your boyfriend taking it off.
Sundays will be the day you
put a huge "Do Not Disturb"
on your entire existence.
However, falling out
is something you will always do alone.
Those are the pictures
that don't make it to Instagram.
That one person,
the person who knocked down your wall
of insecurities, trust issues, and broken promises,
the one who promised to never leave you,
won't even stick around
to help you clean up the pieces.

"The Great Wall"

"A woman will only be as safe as the barriers she sets up to protect herself from her enemies."

W hat is the most valuable thing you own? Where do you keep it? You keep your money in a bank, you keep your jewelry in a box, and you keep your documents in a safe—all to protect them, right? Nobody ever complains about them being there, right? You're almost considered crazy for not having these things to protect your valuables.

Now let's talk about "famous" people. Your favorite actor or actress probably has a bodyguard. Your favorite rapper or singer probably has a few. The President of the United States has the Secret Service, made up of about 3,200 people. All of these people have these measures in place to protect them from the world. What do you have?

Sometimes, being a woman is about access. If they can't get to you, they can't hurt you. Throughout the course of your life, you'll develop this wall—the wall may be made up of wisdom, it may be made of fear, or it may be made of pain. The way you live your life will determine what your bricks are made of. For those who haven't built their wall yet, make it of faith—faith that one day you're going to meet a man who is willing to climb over. To the women with those other types of walls, what's done is done. I'm not about to sit here and tell you that, because you have a fifty-five-foot-high wall, you need to tear it down to make yourself more accessible. That's not fair, not to you or your wall. Your wall is your testament. Your wall is your story.

What messes people up after they get hurt is that they want to act like it never happened. They put all their bricks in a pile somewhere and try to hide them, like when you used to clean your room and put a blanket over the clothes. That's wrong. You have those bricks for a reason; maybe God wanted to give them to you because he knew you needed protection, but instead, you think they're scaring some people away. They might be. Those are the same people that, without the wall, would be able to run right up onto your doorstep and break into your home and into your heart before you even knew what hit you. Then, you're going to wish you had that wall.

A lot of times, men come across so many women who don't have any walls—women who don't have any barriers to protect the good from the bad. If you're one of those women, I need you to do yourself a favor and find one. If you have a barrier, find out what it's made of; that way when you meet somebody who you think might be willing to climb over it, at least they might know what it's made of. Under no circumstances, though, are you to give excuses for your wall or try to convince people that your wall isn't as big as it may seem. When you see this happening, I need you to close your door and go back in the house. It's not your job to throw anybody a rope over the top. Your only obligation is to be waiting on the other side.

No woman wants to have a wall up around her heart, her mind, or her body. It's her defense mechanism. It's her way of figuring out who actually wants to put the effort in and climb over. Never be mad at your wall. Never allow a man to make you wish you didn't have your wall. A real man won't mind it. He'll understand that same wall will be what protects both of you when he arrives on the other side.

The more she had to offer, the more he took.
He always knew how to ask.
He didn't always know how to say, "thank you."
He always expected her to "ride,"
Even when he wasn't sure of the destination.
When she questioned his appreciation,
He questioned her loyalty.
Not once did he question his own.
She always knew she would have his back.
The real question was, who had hers?
Relationships are give and take.
If one person is doing all the giving,
While the other is doing all the taking,
The only thing that's really being taken
Is "advantage."
There's a difference between
Holding it down and being held hostage.

Dear Woman,

It's 1 a.m.
You're about three seconds away
from sending a text that you're going to regret
five seconds after you send it.
Because you don't know
whether it's the weather, your hormones,
or the fact that you're just not ready to walk away yet.
So, you've decided to slide your pride to the side.
And all those nights that you stayed up crying to the side.
All to lay side by side with a man
who could be so close that you can feel his heartbeat,
but still so far away
that you can't tell if it still beats for you.
Just remember.
Remember the first time you looked in his phone
and realized you weren't special.
Remember how you used to finish each other's sentences,
now it takes damn near a miracle for him to text you.
Remember how it felt when the second after you fell,
he fell back, and didn't catch you.
What good is giving your goods
to somebody who doesn't respect you?
Don't let sex be an apology that your heart
didn't give your body permission to give.

"After Katrina"

"Anything that was once built can be built again, but why it fell should determine whether or not you should rebuild."

Everybody wants a house on the beach, until the storm comes—the wind, rain, and tide swallow your property and then spit it out, and you move up the coast like nothing ever happened. All you're left with is a pile of memories, soaked in despair. What do you do when your dream house becomes a nightmare? Do you rebuild or run?

You just broke up with your boyfriend. We won't talk about why, just understand that the beach house was your relationship. The storm was the reason. The rebuild is the day he texts your phone asking if you two can "just talk." I want you to think about this beach house. Take a few things into consideration before you reply. You have insurance called self-love. So, it's not like you'll be homeless, because self-love is the ability for you to be at home wherever you go. This insurance company just wrote you a check for the damages plus 20 percent. What do you do?

If you decide to go, get as far away as you can, as quick as you can. If not, every chance you get you're going to ride down memory lane until your car stops at the vacant lot where your house used to be. You won't know whether to spit on it or fall to your knees and cry your eyes out. That's too much pressure. But if you rebuild, you have to make some changes.

A lot of times people go back to the ones they loved and try to pick up where they left off. They try to pretend that the storm never happened, or they try to live in whatever is left of the house that the storm just wrecked. That's not going to work forever.

I get it. You love him. It happens to the best of us. Combine that with the fact that everybody makes mistakes and that people change, as they say, and that you might have had a storm of your own that missed the house, but just barely. You put all that in a blender and mix it up, and you might find a couple dozen reasons to rebuild that house. All I'm saying is when you do, rebuild **up**. Start over—all the way over; I don't care if you two were together for three years or thirty-three. If a storm blew your house down, it wasn't strong enough. So, somewhere in the process, things got shaky. It's time to get it together. If that means not replying to every text message, not answering every phone call, and not ending every conversation with, "I love you," so be it. If you don't make an actual fresh start, all you're doing is trying to make a castle out of debris, which is going to be weaker than the first one. So, do what you have to do if that's what you have to do. Just do it the smart way. If not, depending on the reason for the storm, you just might be asking for lightning to strike twice.

Dear Woman,

Someone will love you just the way you are.
Never apologize for being you.
Apologize when you have to stop being you
 to be with somebody else.
Your job makes you wear a uniform.
Your church makes you wear a uniform.
The club makes you wear a uniform.
Your relationship is the one place on Earth
where you can get naked—
Where you're just as beautiful with pin-curls and a scarf
as you are forty-five minutes after you leave the salon.
When the MAC doesn't keep your face together,
when the wraps don't keep your waist together,
when you just don't feel like wearing a bra,
if the person you're with wants you to look another way,
act another way, talk another way,
then maybe you should walk the other way.
Life is too damn hard already
for you to be with someone who wants you to change
before they even figure out who you really are.
Be you, unapologetically.

Dear Woman,

It's time to make a decision:
You've got to either tell him to love you
or leave you alone.
It can't be both.
The fact that you two still argue
about how much you used to hurt each other
still gives you hope.
So, today, I'm asking you to pick a struggle:
Either pick today to pack up the memories,
or pick today to pick them over everything
and back up all the "I love you."
All these cameos they make in your text messages
aren't doing anything but confusing you.
What good is getting lost in you all over again
if you won't come find me?
While in the process, I'm losing me.
If you're going to wait for somebody else
to give you permission to smile,
you better sell your teeth,
because you're not going to ever use them.

"Reflections"

*"Sometimes, people don't know who
they are until you show them."*

There comes a point in your life and in your relationships when you are going to have to stop talking and start showing people why they don't deserve you. There are some people who don't get the picture until you become the mirror they so desperately need to show them who they are. A lot of people are good at pointing the finger at you for where you fall short and where you need to grow, but when you ask them what they need to work on, their only response is going to be "you." So, it's your duty to show them, if not to save your relationship with them, then to save the relationship they have with themselves or with whomever they might be with in the future. This duty is to be their reflection. A lot of people don't know their stuff stinks until you pick it up and put it in their face.

This is not about being petty or diminishing yourself by descending to their level. It's about doing things in a way that the person you are talking to will understand. It's about giving someone a taste of their own medicine. This can be done in a conversation or through the lack thereof. It can be done in a day, a week, maybe even a month—it all depends on how much time you are willing to invest in making people become better people. It has to be done, though, and who better to do it than someone who knows exactly who they are dealing with?

Too many times, we, good people, swallow our pride, swallow our voices, and swallow our expectations in order to please people who don't please us back. For you, that should end today. You'll be surprised how quickly some people change once you show them who they are and how who they are makes you feel.

"You can't expect people to fix what
they don't know is broken."

The choice is yours whether or not you want to stick around and figure out whether or not they change. That's a conversation between you and your breaking point. My only concern is that you get in the habit of making people better people.

DEAR WOMAN,

Nobody's perfect,

So be the best you possible.

Every pretty woman gets "carried" away, eventually.

I know sometimes it feels like you've had enough.

You start thinking like a man,

wanting to play that game, too.

Baby girl, I can see your halo.

It shines brighter than good sex and the city.

Every man shouldn't have the pleasure

of tasting your brown sugar.

Keep scribbling in that notebook

and waiting for your Prince Charming.

There's a thin line between

being drunk in love and obsessed.

Every diamond doesn't make it out

of the rough or the players' club.

Some get in too deep.

I know you're waiting to exhale. It's coming.

Remember, the real scandal

is when you start asking yourself,

what's love got to do with it?

So, make sure your Mr. Big is Just Wright,

not just Something New,

before you allow him to claim your baggage

at the airport after you two have jumped the broom.

Dear Woman,

Don't let love destroy your soul.
This love thing isn't as easy
as some people make it seem.
Sometimes,
the happy endings are only in the movies.
Sometimes,
the only one who puts in the effort is you.
Sometimes,
as much as you want it to work, it just won't.
So, I need you to do me a favor.
Don't let it break you.
Try loving yourself more.
Create a happiness on your own
that doesn't require another person
to make you feel like you need their permission.
Be so busy falling in love with yourself
that you don't need anybody else.
Love will come and go.
The key is,
don't let it take a piece of you with it
when it leaves.

"Save Some for the Good Guy"

"The last thing you'll want to have happen is for love to show up with its hand out, and for you to have nothing to give."

Pretty soon, you're not going to have anything left to give. You'll have passed yourself around like a collection plate...like the flu...like a bag of potato chips at a party, using all of the gifts God blessed you with, except for the one you have the most of: a brain.

"If everybody who had a piece of you kept it, when true love finally showed up, what would you have left to give? Besides excuses?"

Sometimes, you can be too good for your own good: too ready, too willing, too able...too hungry to please a man who hasn't proved that he is thirsty for you, when all you needed to do was keep your food in the freezer and wait. Pretty soon, someone would have come along wanting dinner, not just a snack. All I want to know is, why?

Why do you find it so easy to put yourself in so many positions where everything from your morals to your flexibility are tested? Why do you allow yourself to come to a point where you don't even care anymore? When did it become acceptable to let a different bully steal your lunch money every semester? Sometimes one man comes into your life and turns the whole thing upside down. Everything you built will be gone. That's a tragedy.

What isn't a tragedy is when you leave your front door open like you're running a soup kitchen—letting in everything from flies to the wind. There is no excuse for that.

Many a woman is destroyed completely by love one single time. The good thing is that, in the midst of the devastation, she will find her strength, and she will rebuild. The foundation will be much stronger the second time around. My concern is for the woman who takes small steps into the darkness, the woman who, with every fingerprint she allows a man to leave on her mirror, blurs her vision so badly that when she wakes up one morning, she can't even recognize herself. That's who I'm afraid for: the woman who treats herself like a new Mercedes, but one that doesn't ever make it to the show room floor. She was so anxious to be used that she allowed herself to be sold for parts. Don't let her be you. Have you ever seen a woman beaten so badly that she can't be recognized? How about a heart?

The right man always comes eventually. I'm just scared that when he asks you who you are, you won't even know anymore.

DEAR WOMAN,

The scariest part about loyalty
is the fact that, no matter how loyal you are,
if who you're loyal to is not as loyal as you,
your loyalty will always be your downfall.
When they can't answer your question,
they'll question why you asked them.
When you ask for more, you'll be called selfish.
When you ask for better, you'll be called greedy.
When you ask for reciprocity,
they'll ask you for a dictionary.
Instead of constantly asking someone
why they can't be loyal back to you,
ask yourself
why you're being loyal in the first place.

DEAR WOMAN,

Sometimes, a good man is like a parking spot –
a parking spot that is a block away from your door,
when it's raining, and you've got ice cream
in the backseat of your car.
He might not be "perfect," but he's ready for you.
Perfect is a word that cheats so many people out of real.
It cheats them out of good enough to get the job done.
Now you can keep circling the block if you want to,
waiting to find something closer.
You have to ask yourself, are you being lazy?
One day, you're going to turn that corner
and that spot is not going to be there either.
Then that spot would have been perfect, too.
The only person you can be upset with is you.
When you take things for granted,
the things you're granted get taken.
We are all crazy.
We just need to find people
who are our kind of crazy.
So, when we act crazy,
we won't seem crazy.

*One day you're going to **wake up** and she's going to be **gone**.*

*Then you'll have to ask yourself **when** did she really leave?*

__Most__ men don't chase a woman until she's halfway down the block.

*A **real** one won't let her leave the house.*

DEAR WOMAN,

Sometimes "too" can be the loneliest number.
When your heart tells you
that you're too in love to walk away.
but your self-esteem and friends tell you
that you're being treated "too single" for you to stay.
When you're too loyal. Too forgiving.
Too willing to settle for someone
who has shown you too many times
how two people can be in the same relationship.
sleep in the same bed,
but emotionally be two thousand miles apart.
You're too tired to argue but have too much hope.
You've waited too long for a person to change things—
things you consider too easy to even be arguing over.
Remember this:
Being in love is optional, too,
especially to be in it with someone
who is too selfish to treat you like a priority.

DEAR WOMAN,

He's going to come.

The one who's going to make you feel

like everyone else was just practice.

The one safe enough to show your girlfriends.

Smart enough to show your mother.

Strong enough to show your flaws.

He'll love your mind first.

Heart second.

Body always.

He'll prove to you that trust isn't just a word.

That love isn't just a feeling.

That boyfriend isn't just a title.

The only question is, "Will you be ready?"

There is nothing worse than having a king on your doorstep

while you're in bed with a joker.

It's alright to "like "somebody.
Just like them with your eyes open.
When you live inside of a bubble for an extended period of time
because you were hurt,
because you're "focusing on your career,"
or because you've just given up on men,
it's natural that when you finally do meet someone
who gets more than five minutes of your attention,
or shows at least an ounce of genuine interest,
those walls will come tumbling down.
But first, ask yourself, what are you ready for?
What can you handle? and what is your limit?
Believe it or not, you're in a position of vulnerability,
and that and his aggression mixed together
could be a gift or a curse.
You have been so defensive when it comes to men.
You built this crazy wall and someone actually climbed over it.
So, now, you've got butterflies—that's not a bad thing.
But you're going to fall! That's guaranteed.
I can hear it in your texts.
You just have to make sure:
(1) He's going to catch you or (2) You're going to catch yourself.
If not, I wouldn't even start tripping.

DEAR WOMAN,

Have you ever walked into a shoe store

and seen a pair of shoes that you just had to have?

You asked for them in a size eight,

but they only had a seven and a half.

You tried them on, but they just didn't fit.

You knew that you could probably wear them,

but they weren't comfortable.

No matter how you turned and twisted your feet,

they just didn't fit.

You thought about buying them anyway,

though the beauty of the shoe wasn't worth

the pain they would have caused your feet.

So, you just politely said, "No, thank you," and walked away.

Okay, now imagine if that "shoe" was a "man,"

and the "foot" was your heart?

Why is it different?

DEAR WOMAN,

When you want more, ask for more.
If you don't,
you're only hurting yourself in the long run.
When you have feelings for a person
and you don't say anything
because you're "too scared
that it might mess everything up,"
you've already messed up.
You're not only cheating yourself,
you're cheating your future.
Let's say this was a job.
Right now, you're just a volunteer.
No commitment. No future. No security.
The way your life is set up,
the way everyone's life is set up,
you need to be in a permanent position.
Now, you can wait for your "boss"
to offer you a full-time position.
Maybe they will, maybe they won't.
Or
you can walk into their office and say,
"You know what? I need a job
with benefits, responsibilities, and compensation."
The longer you keep working for free,
the harder it is going to be for someone to pay you.
Especially if it is one of those
"friends with benefits" situations;
those benefits will become your biggest liability.

Dear Woman,

Sometimes, saying "I'm all right" is just easier.
Easier than saying, "I don't love myself like I used to,
because somebody I'm still in love with doesn't love me
liked they used to, and I'm not taking it well."
Sometimes, saying "I'm all right" is easier.
Easier than saying, "I spent three hours in the mirror
getting ready for a date last night,
only to be taken to dinner, out for drinks,
and if it wasn't for the fact that my period was on,
I probably would have gotten raped last night."
Apparently, a kiss on the cheek
isn't enough for a first date anymore.
Sometimes, saying, "I'm all right" is easier.
Easier than saying, "I was pregnant with a baby
by a man who said he wanted me but not a baby.
When they took the baby,
I guess I took it too hard, so he left, too.
Now I wish that day in the clinic
I had aborted him and not the baby."
Sometimes, saying, "I'm all right" is easier.
Easier than saying, "I love my son, but I hate being a mother.
Well, maybe I just hate being a single one
because, out of all the dreams
that I had about being a mother,
this wasn't in a single one."

DEAR WOMAN,

Love is like the weekend.

Friday nights, you get all dressed up.

Perfect makeup, perfect shoes, perfect hair.

Perfume that smells like, "I want you to eat me alive,"

accompanied by an attitude that whispers in his ear:

"You'll have to work for it first."

He will spare no expense to impress you.

He'll probably never be more on time in his life.

His car, as clean as the day he bought it.

Favorite shirt, favorite jeans, fresh haircut.

Every flaw covered, every asset exposed.

It's the most beautiful you both will ever look

until your wedding day.

Also, probably the most fake.

No job gives you a list of reasons to quit

in the beginning—only benefits.

So why should people?

Anyway.

You'll spend most of the night

explaining how you're amazing,

and everyone else you dated in the past

just didn't realize it.

The only thing cornier is that they'll say, "Me too."

If things go perfectly, it will last

well into the night.

You never really know who you're dealing with

until Saturday morning.

If the thought of waking up next to them

doesn't completely scare the hell out of you

five seconds after you open your eyes,
you'll stick around.
You'll spend the entire day being normal.
You'll do all the things that life
always seemed to get in the way of.
Like art museums, amusements parks,
and sightseeing tours
in a city you've lived in all your life.
Then, your evening will overlap with the things
that look weird when you do them alone.
Like going to the movies at 7 p.m.
Eating dinner outside.
Public displays of affection.
You will be happier
than seeing the light on at Krispy Kreme,
than finding a WaWa at 3 a.m.
and a cop turning his lights on
and speeding up behind you,
only to fly past you, on his way to pull over
the asshole who cut you off a mile back,
although you had a little too much to drink.
You'll feel like the Real MVP.
And Sunday—
Sunday, you will spend praying
that it never ends.
Only for Monday to come,
and it's back to reality again.
You know why?
The only thing promised in love
is that it will end.
You just have to make sure your weekends last a lifetime.

Thank You.

Thank you for believing in me and supporting what I do.

Thank you for giving me the opportunity to live my dream, while helping make one or two of yours come true.

Thank you for your time.

I want to tell you that I'm proud of you, for everything you've done right and everything you're still working on. It's important that you understand there is somebody here rooting for you. Somebody who wants you to succeed in everything you do.

Whether it be love, life, or the perfect mixture of both.

I hope that, after you close this book, you will be in a better place than when you opened it.

I hope we will meet one day.

But if not,

"No matter how many times the world changes what it means to be a woman, you never stop being a woman in it."

Keep in Touch.

Contact info:

Website: *www.justmikethepoet.com*
Email: *Mike@justmikethepoet.com*
YouTube: *www.youtube.com/justmikethepoet*

Social Media:

Instagram: *@justmike_*
Twitter: *@justmikethepoet*
Facebook: *Just Mike*
Tumblr: *justmikethepoet*

Interested in writing your own book?

Dreams On Paper Entertainment Publishing
"Your Story, Our Help"

Website: *www.dopepublishing.com*
Email: *info@dopepublishing.com*

What's to Come...

This is definitely not my last book.

I love writing too much.

I have a passion to do so that supersedes almost everything else I do.

Right now, though, I have another burning desire.

I can't speak on it too much, but if it's everything I think it will be, then I should be seeing many of you really soon.

Until then, make sure to catch the #justwordstour when it comes to your city.

Make sure you subscribe to my newsletter @ justmikethepoet.com so you can keep in touch with everything I'm working on.

Until then, stay safe, stay happy, and stay a woman.

The End

Michael E. Reid

Michael E. Reid is a poet, author, speaker, and publisher from Philadelphia, Pennsylvania. Michael's story started when, after a failed relationship and unsuccessful suicide attempt, he found himself in a hospital bed with a heavy heart and a blank composition book. What started out as writing therapy for a man who had lost his way exploded into one of the largest movements inspired by contemporary poetry of our time.

Mike used his newfound talent as a writer to establish a social media platform dedicated to the inspiration, enlightenment, and encouragement of women. Five years out from his first poem, Mike has penned four books: *Just Words*, *Just Words II*, *Dear Woman*, and *The Boyfriend Book*. As of summer, 2017, Michael's digital and print sales have ballooned to 250,000 copies sold. To date, Mike has reached over 200,000 women across three social platforms as "Just Mike The Poet."

Mike is always dedicated to giving his supporters what they want. He began by doing one-off poetry performances in and around his hometown, and soon found that small spoken word cafes and restaurants would be jam-packed during his appearances even without much marketing or outreach at all.

Mike, together with "Vision" (Perry Divirgilio) and Jamarr Hall, set out to create a poetry showcase of their own. This resulted in three tours that encompassed over twenty cities in three years— stretching from San Francisco to South Beach, Miami. Over three tours, more than 50,000 people attended. In total, Mike has appeared at over 160 independently organized events in thirty-three cities and five countries around the world. He also has spoken and performed at over twenty colleges and universities. Mike has been on dozens of panels, facilitated workshops, delivered tear-jerking keynote speeches, and volunteered at a local female juvenile treatment facility.

Mike's publishing company, D.O.P.E. Publishing, specializes in teaching rather than taking from his clients. Since its inception in 2014, Mike has facilitated the publication of forty-four books for other authors. Combined, his authors have sold 100,000 books in their own right since Mike dedicated the life he almost lost to other people.

DOPE PUBLISHING

CONSULTING | CREATING | PRINTING
PROMOTION | PUBLISHING

D.O.P.E. (Dreams On Paper Entertainment) specializes in EVERY aspect of publishing. What separates D.O.P.E. from other DIY companies is its comprehensive and all-inclusive list of services, with clients learning the ins and outs of the publishing process. Furthermore, in most cases, D.O.P.E.'s clients will keep 100% of their royalties.

Here at D.O.P.E., our goal is to assist you throughout the entire process of successful self-publishing, while minimizing cost and maximizing your potential for success.

START YOUR JOURNEY
DOPEPUBLISHING.COM

JUST MIKE TRILOGY

Don't miss the opportunity to own all three published works by
Michael E. Reid, a.k.a. Just Mike The Poet. The Just Mike Trilogy
features *Just Words*, *Just Words 2*, and *Dear Woman*. This trilogy is
for a limited time only!

Available now.